T,

MW01297831

i Walter Book Club,

Thank you
for reading.

J.R. Veston

aka

Logan Pierce
xxx

Printed in the USA

ISBN 978-1-5482332-4-2

Graphic Design by Lucas Taccardi

Cover Art by Phil Anderson Blythe
THEOHUXXX ART

Author Photograph by Rob Himebaugh

While primarily a work of non-fiction, many names and identifying features have been altered, and time and space has been condensed for artistic purposes.

CONTENTS

One should judge a man mainly from his depravities.
Virtues can be faked. Depravities are real.

- Klaus Kinski

Between the Sheets

Rise of a Working Stiff

COMING UP

01

I was eight years old when I first saw sex on TV. It was during an episode of *Baywatch*.

On screen, a greying middle-aged man and a curvaceous twenty-something kiss and make-out in an oversized Jacuzzi attached to a salt-water swimming pool. They sip champagne as dawn approaches, cotton-candy skies painted across the horizon.

The woman climbs to the edge of the Jacuzzi and dives into the pool. She emerges, steam rising from her slicked back hair. "Well, what're you waiting for?" she says.

The man eagerly jumps into the refreshing water to join his mistress treading near the deep-end ladder.

Inspired, he says, "I haven't felt this alive in years."

She whispers back, "Kiss me under the water."

They embrace and sink below the surface, their bodies intertwined.

Lost in the throes of it all, the man fails to notice the woman's arm slowly reaching behind him toward the ladder to reveal a pair of tucked away handcuffs. She snaps one bracelet around the bottom rung, and the other around his wrist. She pulls away as he suddenly realizes what's been done. Panic drains the color from his face. He screams and thrashes, the fear bulging through his eyeballs, his face trapped mere inches from salvation.

The woman climbs out of the pool and wraps herself in a towel, finishing her champagne and watching his final moments of life with a cold stare of satisfaction.

Cut to: Me sitting in my parent's living room clutching a juice-box, my jaw hanging and my eyes wide. That image burned into my mind forever.

My first introduction to sex, and it ended with death. Leave it to a trashy daytime drama to let me know the exact moment my childhood was over.

02

It was the year 1999 when my older brother Joey moved out of our shared bedroom and into the basement. Our dad, a disciplined carpenter, had remodeled it into a junior apartment so Joey could save money while commuting to college in the city.

Ten year-old me thought it was an awesome idea. Now I could set up *Hot-Wheels* tracks all over *my* room or leave *Lego* creations sprawled across the floor without the fear of Joey accidentally stepping on them and then pounding me for it. His punishment of choice was to pin me to the ground and crack my toes, yanking them one by one. He was sometimes a jerk to me, but I still looked up to him. Like most boys my age, I wanted nothing more than to be like my older brother.

So, even though I had a room to myself, I spent most of my time in the basement with Joey, usually playing video games or watching TV.

Sometimes his friends would come over and I'd pretend not to eavesdrop on conversations about skipping class, drinking beer, and hooking up with girls.

One night, Joey and I were in his room watching *WWF Raw*, eating water ice and drinking cans of soda.

"I'm going to teach you a little trick," he said, grabbing my *Luigi's* cup and jamming his spoon into the middle of it. "First, you drill all the way to the bottom." He did just that, eating the excess water ice as he dug deeper.

"Hey!" I said. "Don't eat it all."

"Shut up, you'll like this," he said, hitting the plastic bottom. He cracked open a can of *Pepsi* and poured it into the hole. "You fill it up and you got yourself a soda slush."

He handed it back and I took a scoop. "Hey, its pretty good," I said.

"I told you," he said. "That's water ice *Philly* style." He chugged the rest of his can and then cracked a new one. Ringside, Jerry "The King" Lawler went wild, and Joey turned his attention back to the TV. "This is it," he said. "Time for Mr. Socko!"

"You think he's got The Rock beat?" I asked.

"Damn right," he said. "Come on, give him the mandible claw, baby!"

Fixated on the action, Joey cheered and pounded his fists against the ancient wooden chest in front of his TV that served as a makeshift coffee table. Once upon a time, the chest was an heirloom our parents had salvaged from an estate sale. It used to be white, but after watching the movie, *Hook*, Joey decided to paint it blood red. Then he started calling it "The Boo Box, " always threatening to lock me in it if he ever caught me snooping around.

But that, of course, only excited my curiosity.

Friday night while he was out with his friends I decided to open up the boo box and peek inside. There were video game cartridges, cassettes, cd's, and a small collection of movies.

There was also one unmarked black VHS with no sleeve or any identifiable logos or labels. The mystery was intriguing; something inside me desperately wanted to know what was on that tape. I don't know what came over me, but I just had to find out, so I closed the bedroom door, popped it in the VCR, and with my senses piqued, I pressed play.

I stared in awe as the movie's title card flashed in bold and bright neon letters: "**The X-Rated Adventures of Peeping Tom**."

The picture faded in to reveal two pairs of tanned and topless blonde babes playing volleyball on a beach, their glistening bodies on full display. Soon the game ended and the girls got completely naked, deciding against playing more volleyball in favor of playing with each other, kissing, licking, and fingering. Then half a dozen men entered the scene, abs flexed and members throbbing, the girls welcoming them with open arms, open mouths, and spread legs.

I saw things I never thought possible. I didn't know what I was watching. Hell, I didn't know movies like this even existed. All I knew was that I liked it. A lot. All sex and no death; Peeping Tom revolutionized everything.

03

After that day, I was always sneaking into Joey's room to watch the tape. I couldn't get enough. I was given a small taste and now I was hooked. I wanted more—needed more—so I investigated every corner of his bedroom.

I lifted his mattress and found a dirty ashtray with a dozen stubbed out cigarettes. "*Ohh*, Mom's gonna kill you," I mused, picking up one of the butts and re-lighting it with a nearby *Bic*, only to inhale ashen filter and nearly choke to death.

I dumped out Joey's backpacks and dug through his bureau. To my surprise, I found a tattered erotic novel hidden in the back of his underwear drawer. I cracked it open and eagerly consumed all of the steamy and graphic stories; words like "Cock," Pussy," "Blowjob," and "Doggy style" offered context to what I was watching on the tape, causing my sexual imagination to surge.

When I was eleven and on the precipice of puberty, I started masturbating—*jacking off*—as it was referred to in the novel, but there was never any finish for me, no orgasm; it was more like tugging a rubber band until I got bored. I doubt my body was even producing *cum* at that age, but nevertheless, I couldn't keep my hands away.

Admittedly, I was afraid to jack off, which must've been due to the Irish Catholic guilt sinking in. Every Sunday in my CCD class I was lectured on the importance of abstinence and the sinful nature of sex, pornography, and masturbation; meanwhile I'd be fantasizing about the girls in my class, their short summer dresses, and us sneaking away to the confessional for a little reconciliation. In fact, the only thing I can remember actually praying for was to not be called on and have to stand at the blackboard with a raging boner.

At a young age, I quickly learned the arresting power of my libido. All I could *ever* think about was jacking off, and it didn't take long for me to lose control.

At home, I'd take any excuse to hide away and tug myself—usually locked in my bedroom or the hall bathroom with my ear pressed against the door. I'd give myself twelve or so pumps and then stop to make sure nobody was nearby. With the coast clear, I'd go another twelve and then stop and listen; rinse and repeat. The act alone gave me such a rush from the fear of getting caught. I became so in-tune, I could determine someone's distance and what room they were in by the creak of the floorboards beneath their feet.

When I was twelve, *"AOL"* was a household name, and I was constantly searching the web for porn. Under the guise of doing homework, I would sit at my parent's desktop computer, cautiously looking over my shoulders as I typed the *naughty* keywords to get what I craved. My reward came in the form of low-resolution photos or short 10-second video clips, barely enough to satisfy my hunger. I'd stay plugged in for hours. I wanted it all, whatever I could find, whatever was free, and most importantly, whatever was easily deleted from the search history.

Nights when Joey was out and after my parents had gone to bed I would log into AOL under a Guest account and join "Adult" chat rooms with names like, "Twenty-Something's," "At the Bar," "One Night stands," and "BBW's"— the definition of which eluded me. Conversations began with three simple letters; the acronym, A/S/L—Age, Sex, Location, an effective tool to gauge whether or not a real-life hook up was possible, but that never happened for me.

At least not until the advent of *Myspace*, that is.

04

The year was 2004, it was winter, and I was fifteen years old.

Joey had officially moved out of our parent's house and into the city, so, naturally, I moved into his old room in the basement. He was kind enough to leave behind the Boo-Box, but unfortunately he took the tape with him. It didn't really matter, though, because by now, I, and everyone else, had long since forgotten about VHS.

For Christmas, my parent's bought me my first laptop. It was bulky and the processor was sluggish, but it was mine and it allowed me the freedom to meticulously explore the underbelly of the Internet from the safety and privacy of my bedroom.

Outside of porn, MySpace was my primary hub of online entertainment. I spent most of my time after school logged in, perfecting my profile, finding new friends, searching for music to listen to, or new movie trailers to watch.

While scrolling through the friends list of one of my favorite local bands—*Westdale*—I stumbled upon the profile picture of a girl smoking a cigarette while wearing fishnets, a plaid skirt, a torn black t-shirt, and layers of smoky makeup. I clicked on her page and learned her name was Lily. She was sixteen years old, of Korean descent, and went to high school in a neighboring district. Her bio listed her height at four-feet-eleven inches, "fun sized," as she called it, but I preferred a different nickname. I liked to think of Lily as a *Spinner*, the definition of which I learned by frequenting my then-favorite porn site, the infamous, *"CumFiesta.Com."*

I sent Lily a friend request and wasted no time in introducing myself.

Cursory dialogue:

Me: "OMG ur so hot."

Lily: "Wow, thanx. U too qt <3."

At that age, I was going through a wannabe rocker phase and was the acting drummer in a mediocre-at-best metal-core band, so I played the musician card to my advantage. I offered to teach Lily how to play drums, insinuating, *I'm sure you can handle a stick.* I sent her a photo of me in my parent's garage, sitting shirtless behind my drum kit, sweaty after an exhausting band practice.

She responded with a photo of her wearing a jade corset and black panties with the message, "Oh, I bet I can teach *U* a few tunes."

This carried on until one night I decided it was time to act, so I developed a plot. Together, Lily and I would skip school and she would take an early morning train from her neighborhood to mine. I'd meet her at the station and lead her back to my house while my parents were away at work; they maintained the same schedule for years, so I knew their routine well. Getting away with it would be a cinch.

I pitched this to her and she went for it.

"How about next week?" I asked.

"Why wait?" she quipped. "How about tomorrow?"

"Tomorrow?"

"If you think you're up to it," she said, baiting me.

"Oh, you're bad," I said. "Fine. Tomorrow it is."

"Good boy," she said with authority.

It all seemed so easy; the fantasy came natural. I had been watching and reading about scenarios like this for years, and now it was finally time to actually make it a reality. And the best part was, I wouldn't have to sneak into her house and risk getting chased away naked by an angry dad with a shotgun or an overzealous grandmother with a butchers knife. Instead, Lily was coming to me, entering into my domain, my world.

And there, down in the basement, under the covers and between the sheets, I'd have my first fuck.

4:30 a.m. My dad woke, made a pot of coffee, and read the newspaper.

5:15 a.m. He grabbed his Philadelphia Flyers vanity keychain and went out to start his green Dodge 4x4, heating the interior and de-icing the windshields.

5:30 a.m. Fully dressed and ready for work, my mom came downstairs and had herself a cup of steam.

6:00 a.m. My dad drove her to the train station so she could catch her train into the city for her job at the hospital. Then he drove to his job site in Tinnicum Township.

7:00 a.m. I woke up, showered, gelled my hair, and dressed in an extra tight pair of black pleather pants I wore last year for my *Eric Draven* Halloween costume; I liked them because they showed off my package. Then I spritzed *Axe* body spray around the basement to set the mood.

7:45 a.m. I left the house and trekked over the salted sidewalks of Michigan Avenue onto the plowed streets of Muhlenberg. A quarter mile later I turned left on Swarthmore Ave., heading in the complete opposite direction of my high school.

And that's when I saw the truck approaching: a green Dodge 4x4. Closer still, a silver and orange Philadelphia Flyers vanity front license plate confirmed my fear.

"Shit," I squeaked out, losing my breath.

Desperate for an escape, I dashed behind a parked car and pretended to tie my shoe, holding my breath as the truck neared. I could've sworn I heard the screech of the brakes, but it was only my imagination. He drove on, unaware, and I remained undetected, for now.

But what was I supposed to do? Was he driving back to the house? He must've forgotten something, I reasoned, and he's driving back just for a second to pick it up before heading back out. Surely he wouldn't be there when I got back, my virginity was hanging in the balance here!

For this day to succeed I would have to be crafty. I could lie, I thought. If he's there I could tell him I had a half-day at school and hope he wouldn't catch on to the fact that there would no busses on the streets and no other kids on the sidewalks, just me, home early with a girl he's never met. It was my only option; it would have to work. Only problem was, a half-day meant 11:30 at the earliest, and right now it was barely 8:15.

I pressed on, staggered, but determined.

Twenty minutes later, I met Lily at the train station. She was wearing black combat boots, cream leg warmers, tight black yoga pants, and a grey pea coat; I nearly lost myself imagining what could be hidden underneath.

Before the train even pulled away we jumped each other, hugging, kissing and playfully groping as people gawked from the cabin windows, jealous because we were young and in lust.

Lily asked, "Are your hands cold?"

"Absolutely," I said. "It's freezing."

She grinned. "I know a way we can fix that," she whispered, grabbing my hand and slipping it down the front of her pants. "It's warmer down there."

God, she was a killer, all right.

Hand in hand, we (very) slowly walked to my house, taking plenty of opportunity to detour and wander around town as we flirted and fantasized. Sometime later we ended up in *Pathmark* reading silly birthday cards to each other.

"Hey, Look," I said, pointing to a novelty card with a shirtless male-model on the front. "Pin the junk on the Hunk? Huh."

"What, this junk?" Lily said, suddenly grabbing me and pulling me close. "Stop stalling," she whispered. "I want it now."

"Ye..Yes, ma'am," I said, helpless in her grasp.

She let go and walked away. Instinctively, I followed close behind. Lily had taken control; she was now the one in charge.

I have no idea what time it was when we got to my house, but I know it was still early, and as we approached, I saw my dad's truck parked snugly in the driveway. Dread washed over me.

Warily, I opened the front door and we crept inside. To my advantage, the basement stairs and the living room were on different sides of the first floor, so I encouraged Lily to go downstairs and wait while I cleared the air with my dad.

I took a deep breath and sauntered into the living room playing like everything was as it should be. "Hey Dad, what's up?" I said with shaky confidence.

"Hey..." he said, almost dragging out the word with mild confusion. "What are you doing home?"

"Half day, remember?" I lied, bouncing on the balls of my feet.

"Half-day?" he asked, surprised.

I continued, "Yeah…I told mom, figured she would've told you."

He paused, unsure. "Hm, must've forgot, I guess."

"Ah, well, you know," I said, tiptoeing away. "Okay, well, I'm gonna go down to my room now. Also I have a friend over so it's just going to be the two of us, okay?"

"Sure thing."

"Okay, great," I said, racing downstairs.

Lily had already taken off her boots and was now sitting on my bed anticipating my arrival. I shut my bedroom door, and turned on my TV for background. Then I kicked off my shoes and joined her.

She pulled me in for a kiss and whispered, "Did you want to use a condom?"

I froze. *Condoms?* I had been so clouded from watching graphic, fantastical, and predominantly condom-less porn that I completely overlooked the fact that I should've bought a box. The nerves crept back.

"I don't have any," I sighed. "This is my first time and I—"

"This is your first time?" she said, cutting me off.

Pouting, I nodded my head. "…Uh huh."

"You are *so* cute," she said, leaning in, kissing my cheek and nibbling my earlobe. "Don't worry about it," she said, slipping off her jacket. Underneath, was black lace lingerie with matching thigh-high stockings.

I gazed fixated, hypnotized. My brain effectively shut off as my little head turned on and took the driver seat. With eyes narrow and jaw slack, my breathing regressed into slow and methodical growls. The world around me faded into oblivion, and in that moment the only thing that mattered to me was sex.

My pants suffocated me as I grew, and Lily took notice, biting her lip and running her fingertips along the bulge, causing jolts and spasms like a caged animal charging the bars. She unzipped me and I unfurled into her hands, looking positively huge in comparison. She placed me on her tongue; I barely fit into her mouth, but she didn't seem to mind. She lay on her back and urged me on top.

Trembling, I mounted her and she reached down and slipped me inside. With deep conviction, I thrust as Lily dug her nails into my back, her body contorting.

Less than sixty seconds later, I was on the verge of combustion. And as if she were straight out of the movies herself, Lily asked me to do it all over her face.

"Please," she said. "I want to taste it."

It was everything I ever wanted and more, Lily smiling a mouthful of my pearls.

05

Over the coming years, I remained a product of the Internet. MySpace evolved into *Facebook*. Facebook spawned *Twitter*. Twitter was special for me because it offered something unlike any other social media platform: the freedom to post porn. Twitter is the nucleus of the industry.

I followed profiles of production companies and distributors, receiving up to the minute news on what was hot and current. But more importantly, I followed the profiles of *performers*, giving me a glimpse into the lives of actual porn stars. I quickly learned porn was produced almost exclusively in Los Angeles, and most performers were living comfortably under the warm California sun, earning a healthy paycheck fucking for a living. I wanted that life.

Now, I know what you're probably thinking, and the answer is, NO, I was not a total loser in high school; I didn't spend all of my time jacking off in front of my computer, just most of it. I really liked watching porn and I had an overactive sex drive—sue me! I was an honor's student, I was the treasurer of the drama club, and, believe it or not, I even had a healthy string of relationships throughout my teenage years.

So, now that we're square, let's move on.

When I was sixteen I started jacking off an average of four times a day. I would try to time my shits with my showers so I could spend a lot of time alone in the bathroom without anyone asking too many questions. I'd *Google* while I'd shit, and then I'd run the shower, perch my laptop on the toilet seat in front of me, and sit cross-legged on the tile floor. Some days I was fast about it, and other days I would lose track of time, steam fogging the room and condensation wrinkling the wallpaper.

When I was eighteen I started skimming the escort section of *Backpage*. I was hot on the idea of showing up to a hotel room with a wad of cash in one hand and my dick in the other, being greeted at the door by a willing vixen. This was yet another porno fantasy I had seen time and time again.

Girls my age were fine and all, but after my experiences with Lily, who proved to be a tremendous flash in the pan, my sex-life remained stagnant, uninspired, and sometimes downright fucking boring. I had already earned my associates degree in sex-ed while most of my peers were still studying for their SAT's. I wanted someone new to shock me, someone to fuck me sideways, and at the time the most tangible option in my life were escorts. I mean, come on, they're *professionals*.

Eventually, I worked up the courage to call some of them. With endorphins rushing and my hands shaking,

I opened *YouPorn* and put one of my ear-buds next to the receiver with the volume turned up extra loud so they could hear. I thought it would be a turn-on, but most of them seemed to disagree and hung up almost immediately.

One was amused, though, a dirty blonde by the name of Sierra.

"Wow, it sounds like you're already having one hell of a party," she said. "You want me to sound like that, baby?"

Dry-mouthed, I faltered, "Um...yes. Maybe we can... make an appointment?"

Sierra giggled. "Sure, baby. Just call me a half hour before you wanna come and I'll give you my address."

"You...want me to come?"

"Oh yeah, baby."

"I...I think I'm gonna come right now."

"Um, wait, what?"

And then I did, onto my stomach and in my bellybutton. Regaining my senses, I hung up, turned off my phone, cleared my search history and went to bed without ever calling her back.

06

Following in Joey's footsteps, I went to college in the city, enrolling as a film major at Temple University. But unlike him, I opted to live on campus. I got a job working the projector at the school movie theater. It was a fairly isolating position. I spent most of my weekends alone in the booth threading 35mm prints, eating popcorn and boxes of *Buncha Crunch*. The job was low maintenance, and it put a little extra cash in my pocket, so I couldn't really complain.

In the booth, after threading *Captain America* for a 9 p.m. screening, I killed time on my laptop, clicking between numerous Internet tabs and browsing escort ads; you know, a typical Friday night. I narrowed my choices to a provider who went by the name of *Alice Wonderland*. Physically, Alice was the spitting image of Rooney Mara circa, *The girl with The Dragon Tattoo*. She had jet-black hair, an ivory complexion, tatted skin, and a septum piercing. Daring and dangerous, she did a wonderful job of whetting my appetite.

For little reason other than because I could, I decided tonight would be the night; the first time I visit a pro.

I called Alice and resisted the impulse to subject her to what I was watching. In so many words, I scheduled a midnight appointment, $200 for one hour of safe sex.

Final credits rolled shortly after 11 p.m. I killed the power to the booth, locked up, clocked out, and walked to the campus ATM. I trotted to my dorm, showered, gelled my hair, put on a shirt and tie, and grabbed a handful of condoms. I got into my '98 forest green Nissan Maxima my parents had gifted me for my 18th birthday, and I drove to an *Econolodge* Motel located off the industrial highway.

En route, I was flooded with second thoughts. "What if this is a trap?" Maybe Alice was undercover and I was knee-deep in a sting operation with cops ready to arrest me the second I handed her the money. "Am I a shitty person for doing this?" I'd seen enough Hollywood movies to understand there is something inherently immoral about paying for sex, perhaps even something dehumanizing. But we were two consenting adults. If she enjoyed herself and so did I, what's the problem?

I kept driving. I could worry all I wanted but the truth was, I relished the thrill of being bad.

In the parking lot, I called Alice and she gave me her room number. I locked my car, approached the door, and knocked. Alice opened wearing an oversized and unbuttoned dress shirt that barely covered her glitter speckled chest and her cream-colored panties. She welcomed me in with a light kiss, taking my hand and leading me to the bed.

She asked, "So, what brings you here tonight?"

Fumbling, I said, "Well, I, uh, I don't know, I just wanted to do something…crazy."

"…Crazy?" she asked, intrigued.

"Yeah, I, uh, I want to be bad," I said.

A devious smile crept across her face. "…*Bad*. I can work with this."

The conversation broached business. As per her instructions, I put the cash into an envelope she had handed me. I then placed the envelope on her nightstand. Alice took it and walked into the bathroom, leaving me alone. I kicked off my shoes and loosened my tie, undoing a couple buttons of my shirt along the way.

Two minutes later, Alice emerged, naked. She sauntered toward me, veiled in seduction.

"*Bad*, huh?" she asked, crawling onto the bed. "Like this?" She arched her back, her ass facing me. Looking over her shoulder, she said, "You wanna spank me?"

I rested my hand on her ass and then gave it a light smack.

Alice giggled. "Oh, come on," she said. "I'm sure you can do better than that. Haven't I been a bad girl, daddy?"

"You…want me to hit you harder?"

"*Punish* me."

I smacked her cheek again, and then the other, harder this time. Alice moaned as her skin flushed red.

She crawled over to me. "Give me your hand," she said, taking it and placing it around her neck. "Now squeeze."

"You want me to *choke* you?" I asked.

She gripped my hand, tightening it herself. "Stick your other one in my mouth." I brought it near, hesitating. "Do it," she said, her capillaries protruding. I stuck three fingers in her mouth, and she let them slide over her tongue and down her throat. She stared at me, nodding her head *'yes'* as tears collected in her eyes. Finally, she grabbed my wrist and pulled out my hand. I let go of her neck and she gasped for air, grinning as her makeup ran down her cheek in a thick stripe of black.

"Thank you, Daddy," she said. "Now lie down."

She pushed me on my back, kissing me while undoing my belt. She took down my pants and stroked my ego. "Mm, you have a *fat* cock," she said.

"You think so?"

"I don't know if I can fit it in my mouth...but I can try," she said. "Do you have any condoms, baby?"

"Plenty!" I said, reaching for my pocket. I grabbed one and handed it to Alice. She unwrapped it and slipped it on. Then she used her mouth. It was so warm; my body tingled, my heart raced. It was happening; my fantasy was coming true. Coming. It was coming. I was—*Oh shit.*

I convulsed and filled the latex reservoir, groaning in a bittersweet blend of ecstasy and embarrassment.

Alice waved her finger in disappointment. "Tsk. Tsk. Eager boy."

"Damn it. I'm sorry," I said, defeated.

"I'm only kidding," she said. "I think it's...*cute.*"

"Oh yeah," I sighed. "*Real* cute." Catching my breath I tried to explain myself. "Its just I'm…you're so…and this was…wow."

Alice laughed, took off the condom, and carried it into the bathroom. She returned with a towel and let me clean myself off. Then she crawled back onto the bed and laid her head against my chest.

"I have an idea," she said. "Lie on your stomach."

In lieu of sex, Alice offered me a full body massage for the rest of the hour. With only the sounds of passing traffic and the smearing of cream, the air was mildly awkward, the massage being somehow more personal than the would-be sex.

Alice cleared her throat. "I don't mean this to be rude," she said, "but aren't you a little young to be seeing escorts?"

"I guess so," I said.

"I just mean most of my clients are like middle aged married men."

"I've just always been curious," I said. "I don't know, do you think that's weird?"

"Baby, it takes a lot more than that to weird me out," she said. "I actually think it's kind of cool."

"*Cool?*" I asked.

"Yeah. You know, most guys think about doing it, but you actually had the balls to go through with it. I can respect that."

"Guess I'm the cool pervert then."

"How old are you, anyway?" she asked.

"Nineteen," I said. "And you?"

"Eh, somewhere around there. So, do you go to school?"

"Yeah, I go to Temple."

"Temple!" she said, lighting up. "That's where I wanted to go, but they didn't accept me, so."

"What did you want to study?"

"Well, that was part of the problem. I didn't know what I wanted to do. I still don't, I guess. I took a couple Gen-ed classes at community college, but I don't do well in classrooms, I don't know. What do you study?"

"Film."

"Wow, that's so cool. So do you, like, want to be a director or something?"

"I'm still trying to figure that one out. So, uh, I'm guessing Alice isn't your real name, is it?"

"No."

"I had a feeling. Do you mind if I ask what your real name is?"

"Sure. It's Piper."

"*Piper.* I like that. It's...*cute*," I said.

She playfully slapped my back, "Oh, shut up."

"So, did you mean what you said earlier? About my dick being big, or was that part of the act?"

"I meant it. Trust me. I've seen enough to know and

appreciate a good one when I see it. I'd say it has some serious potential."

"Potential, eh?"

"Sure. But first we need to work on your self-control."

"Oh, ha-ha. You're funny," I said. "You should be a comedian, you know that?"

"Yeah," she said, pondering. "Maybe in my next life.

An alarm went off on her phone. My hour was up. She toweled my back and I got dressed.

"I guess I ought to head out," I said.

"You should keep my number," she said. "Call me if you want to get together sometime—professionally, or, you know, as friends or something."

"Thanks, I'll do that," I said. "It was nice meeting you, Piper."

"Yeah, you too." She walked me to the door and we shared a kiss and a parting hug.

A week later I called her to see if she wanted to come with me to a party near campus, but her number was disconnected; "Sorry, the number you are dialing is unavailable," was all that I heard on the other line, and she had no voicemail set up for me to leave a message. I checked Backpage and all of her ads seemed to have been removed. Like the abrupt bursting of a bubble, Piper had simply disappeared, gone as if she hadn't even existed in the first place, but the memory of her still remained.

07

It should probably come as no surprise that *James Deen* had a **big** influence on my life. He's the porno poster-boy for guys like me: short, handsome, approachable, and decidedly average–the perfect combination to play the common man, the horny teenager, or the all-American. And to top it off, James is packing some serious heat below the belt, and regardless of how trivial the porn plots may be, the end result is always the same: he gets laid and he gets paid.

The access was at my fingertips, so I tweeted him. In 140 characters I declared James as my idol, praising his talent and thanking him for all his hard work. I told him I wanted to be a performer like him. I asked for any help he'd be willing to offer, any advice to get me started. I knew James would sense something comparable between us; how could he not? I remained hopeful and assured he would give me a chance. Maybe he'd even make me his protégé. A boy could hope.

Six weeks went by and James still hadn't responded. He was probably too busy to see a tweet from some random kid in Pennsylvania; it must've gotten lost and fell to the bottom of the proverbial pile. Whatever. Onward and upward.

I didn't need a co-sign from James Deen to get ahead. There were plenty of other male performers on Twitter; I followed at least a dozen of them. I edited minor variations of the James tweet and sent them out, but most of those pleas also went unanswered. All but one.

I heard back from a performer by the name of *Chester Bang.* Chester was fairly new to the industry. I figured this much after checking his Twitter bio, which read, "Been Bangin and Slangin for 3 major *cumpanies* so far. Bangbros, DogFart & DevilsFilm. Who's Next? Call *Sky Models* to Book me now!"

Chester wasn't exactly a guy you would call handsome. Some people would say he's ugly, and others might go on to say he's got a face like a battered mule, and that fact was often reflected in his work. Sure, he may have performed for those companies, but each scene was either a cheap gangbang or a Bukkake.

Chester Bang was decidedly a *mope*—just another anonymous dick doing dirty work for low wages.

In other words, his career was the antithesis of James Deen's, and therefore, the exact opposite of everything I wanted, but I couldn't afford to be picky with the insider information I received; after all, I was looking for advice, not a census.

Chester tweeted me. "Broseph," he said, "you gotta network yourself and get an agent; call Sky Models. They'll hook you up."

An *agent*? I would've never guessed that porn stars had agents. I don't know, the idea of a sex worker having someone book all of their gigs—schedule the sex, and then take a percentage of their earnings struck me as, well, someone more like a pimp. But I soon realized that was me being dense; actors have agents, musicians have agents, writers have agents, even make-up artists have agents, so why shouldn't porn stars?

And since Chester mentioned *Sky Models*, I figured that'd be a good enough place to start. A quick Google search landed me on their homepage, which read, "Sky Models Inc. Where the Air is Crisp, and the Talent is Fresh."

The website was split into two categories, "Male Talent" and "Female Talent," with each page offering semi-nude headshots along with stage names and an accompanying list of acronyms detailing the particular acts he or she is willing to do on camera. Things like: "B/J, B/G, B/B/G, B/G/A, and D/P."

There was also a blinking tab that read, "Become a Model Today!"

The process: Take naked photos and include them in a coherent pitch to the powers that be at Sky Models. It seemed so easy, literally a keystroke away.

I snapped shirtless selfies with one hand resting behind my head and the other one slipped down the front of my pants. I took nudes of myself doused with baby-oil while flexing to accentuate muscle definition, not that I really had much. Finally, I took close-ups of my hard-on while holding it next to a banana for scale; that was my ace in the hole. Then I attached the photos to the model submission page and included my name, my number, and my affinity for porn. I even dropped Chester's name as a reference because, well, it couldn't hurt.

I moved the cursor over the enter key, but my fingers hovered above my laptop's trackpad. I nervously picked at my thumbnail, contemplating. I could be setting myself up for rejection, I thought—shot down straight out of the gate. But this was a necessary first step; having an agent was an integral part of the game, and right now I desperately wanted to play ball. I pressed the button and let out a sigh of relief.

There. Done. No looking back now.

08

Feeling existential in the fall of junior year, I took an eighth of shrooms at a house party in North Philly. After thirty minutes of waiting, I didn't feel anything, so, naturally, I took another. Soon the graffiti stricken walls were pulsating and I sunk deep into the cushions of a dirty couch.

The next thing I remember is my tongue inside of another person's mouth, swirling around with theirs. I cupped their soft face in my hand and slowly pulled away. Looking deep into a pair of button-brown eyes I discovered they belonged to the most beautiful creature I had ever seen.

In a daze, I asked, "What's your name?"

"Allie," she whispered.

"Allie," I said, pulling her lips back to mine. "Do that again."

We shared another moment of bliss before one of her friends came and took her away from my arms and out of reach. Too much too soon, I guess.

Left alone, the drugs started to turn; people around me morphed and mutated into gross caricatures and vile beasts, snarling and foaming at the mouth. Panic set in. I couldn't breath. I lurched off the couch and inertia propelled me against a wall, pitting me face to face with my reflection in a hallway mirror. I froze in white terror at what I saw.

This was bad, very bad.

Someone bumped into me and broke my trance, giving me the strength I needed to navigate the muck and lumber outside where I dropped to my knees and puked in the gutter. Delirious, I discovered the world had erupted in flame, ephemeral demons dancing in the rising black smoke. Arrested by terror, I fell to the ground, my back against the cold concrete. Mouth agape, I stared at the spirits until my eyes burned, white ash billowing all around, encasing me.

But suddenly, out of the fires arose an angel, her wings silhouetted by glowing amber. She was coming; rapture was upon me.

Then darkness. Black out. Curtains.

I woke in a stranger's apartment amidst half a dozen outstretched and bare-skinned bodies strewn across a couch and the living room floor. I looked down by my side and there she was, Allie, nestled in my arms. I couldn't believe it. I have no idea how I got there or how we came to be together, but I didn't care; having her now was what's important, and although I couldn't be sure, something inside told me she was the one who had kept me safe last night. It was because of her that I survived.

Allie: my guardian angel.

I ran my fingers through her long brunette hair just to make sure she was really there and that I wasn't still hallucinating. She stirred, her soft waking eyes meeting mine. I felt a calming warmth in my stomach, and for the first time, I was in love.

Allie was in her third year at U-Penn, studying to be an English teacher. She also worked part-time as a server at a restaurant in Rittenhouse Square. I'd go in every so often to grab a drink and hang out whenever she was on. Sometimes I would go just to watch her work. There was something so attractive about the way she interacted with customers; she was tenacious in securing a good tip.

After long shifts, her skin would carry a lingering scent of the kitchen, a curious mix of smoke and grease. Most guys would have probably asked her to shower, but I savored it, the smell of a hard day's work.

Around the time Allie and I became exclusive, I learned that Temple was offering a study away program for film majors, giving us a chance to study for a semester in the epicenter of American film production. The opportunity was there, beckoning, so I applied.

Two weeks later, I received my letter of acceptance. Starting in January, I would be living alongside nineteen other students at the Oakwood Apartments, right next to the Warner Brothers lot. I'd have a full 16-credit course load and an internship at a new-media studio called, *Veneer Pictures*, which specialized in producing low-budget features that were then released episodically online. I had never heard of them before, but it sounded like the perfect place for a budding filmmaker to get his feet wet.

Either way, I didn't much care; all that mattered was I now had my ticket to L.A.

09

Allie and I were at Longwood Gardens, admiring the perennials in the orchid house when I got a call from an unknown number with an area code I didn't recognize.

"*818?*"

"I think that might be a California number," Allie said. "Could be someone from the program."

"It could. Or it could be Comcast trying to scam me with a new deal."

"You never know."

Usually, I would've just let this call go to voicemail— "I'll get to it later," I'd say with no intention of actually doing so, but not this time. I answered, and a husky voice on the other line identified himself as *Max Michigan*.

"*Who?*" I asked.

"Max. Michigan," he said, clearing his throat. "I own Sky Models. You sent in some photos."

Holy shit. In light of recent events I had almost completely forgotten I'd applied. I lowered my voice and changed tact so Allie wouldn't hear. "Oh, yes, hi, sir, thanks for call—"

"Yeah, Yeah, So, kid," Max said. "If your photos are anything to judge by, you definitely got the right tool for the job, know what I mean?"

"Wow, thank you." I said, surprised. "So, uh, do you think you'll represent me?"

"Whoa, hold on there, chief," Max said. "I ain't gonna put you on the site or nothing—not yet, at least. What I can do is *hip pocket* you and toss you one or two gigs. If you do well, we can talk papers. 10% for me either way."

"Um, well, what kind of scenes?"

"Basic P.O.V. Boy/Girl shit. Easy stuff. Pay is three hundred per. What do you think?"

Stammering, I said, "Uh, well, I—"

"Do you want it or not, kid?"

This was it, the pieces coming together to form as one, my chance right in front of my face, just waiting for me to reach out and grab it. If only...

"...Yes. Yes, I want it."

"Are you *sure*?" he asked, pressing.

"Absolutely," I said. "This has been a dream since I was a kid. I'm sure."

"Rock and roll," he said. "Call me when you're in town and I'll put you to work."

"Definitely," I said. "Thank you, Max."

"Oh, one more thing," he said. "Get yourself a good stage name."

He hung up. Allie stared at me, confused, vulnerable. "Who was that?" she asked.

I hesitated. I knew this would be a deciding moment. Nothing would complicate a relationship quite like porno aspirations.

"We should go back to the car," I said.

On the ride home, I confessed everything. Allie wasn't offended or dismissive, but she couldn't understand my motivation, and I couldn't seem to offer her a reasonable explanation; I don't even know if I had one for myself. I wanted to articulate why I was so drawn to porn and why I was so willing and unafraid to dive in head first, but I couldn't. Not yet. All I knew was that if I didn't at least try, the rest of my life would be the plagued by the question of "What if?"

I could only offer apologies. I assured her it wouldn't affect the way I felt about her, and I promised that if I could, I'd make enough money to fly her out anytime she wanted. I convinced her to stay with me because we were hopeful, we were idealistic, and we were in love.

"And it won't be cheating," I said, "it'll just be *work*."

10

I thought of what Max had said. I still didn't have a stage name. It's a task I guess I'd been avoiding. I mean, a name is everything; it's a brand, it's an identity, and it's a major fucking responsibility. I wanted something powerful and striking, but also inviting and casual. And I wanted Allie to be involved in the process; I thought it would help give her a greater sense of security if we were open and worked together as a team.

We brainstormed:

"How about, *Guy Pierce*?" I asked.

"Like the actor?" she said.

"Like my favorite actor," I said. "Except, I would change the name to spell P-I-E-R-C-E. You see? Double entendre."

"Ah, Piercing like a knife," she said.

"*And* like a cock," I said, flexing my arm in front of my crotch.

"*Funny,*" she said, unamused. "Pierce is fine, but I'm not too crazy about the name, Guy, though. It feels so impersonal, you sound like a prop."

"I think a lot of time that's pretty much what the guys are," I said.

"See—*Guy.* You'd just be another "one of the guys." Another random penis."

"You think it sounds too porny," I said.

"Too porny or too corny?" she asked. "And is there even a difference? Anyway, you'd probably get sued by the actor or something, right?"

"I never thought about that," I said.

"You know what name I love?" she said.

"What?"

"*Logan.* I've never met anyone named Logan before, but I just love the way it sounds; it rolls off the tongue."

"*Logan,*" I said, imagining lights on a marquee. "Logan…Pierce, Male Performer. Kind of has a ring to it."

"Sounds almost sophisticated," she said.

"Like the kind of guy who'd take you out to the ballet and then bang you in the back of a dark alleyway. Ha! Logan Pierce. I like it."

"Good," she said, pulling me in for a kiss. "Now get out there and make it."

And just like that, I was given a name.

Logan Pierce was born.

11

Most students accepted into the program fly to Los Angeles with a round-trip ticket, fully intent on promptly returning after the semester ends, the call of the western tide proving only temporary, but not me.

I decided to road trip, overstuffing my 98' Maxima with everything I owned, driving west with the certainty that I was going there to stay. For four days and three nights I pounded 5-Hour energy drinks and ate nothing but CLIF Bars as I crept along the flat and mostly barren landscape of the I-40 highway, save for the vast rolling clouds of the New Mexico sky and the green inferno that is Flagstaff. I stopped only to use the bathroom or turn in at unquestionably ratty motels. The drive was solitary and lonely, but with every passing mile I felt stronger and more independent, the tether to home slowly being cut.

On the morning of The January 17th, I crossed the Los Angeles County line. First thing I noticed were the outlying mountain ranges that practically encapsulated the city, undulating waves of stone stretched as far as I could see.

My first task was to drive through Hollywood—the supposed core of it all. Getting off the 101 freeway, I drove along Hollywood Blvd and quickly realized it was not a place for celebrity like the movies had promised. Instead, it seemed to be filled with nothing but tourists and homeless, but being that I briefly satisfied both criteria, I felt welcomed.

I called Max and he told me to meet him at his office, which was located in the depths of the San Fernando Valley in a town called Chatsworth. If I thought Hollywood was grim, Chatsworth was a relative wasteland; I saw nothing but chain restaurants, decrepit warehouses, and not one stitch of green grass, but aesthetics aren't everything, right?

The Sky Model's office was located in a small strip-mall off Topanga Blvd. There were no sign and the windows were blacked out. I knocked on the door and from the other side a voice called out, "It's fucking open!"

Max operated Sky Models out of a one-room office cast in fluorescent light. In the room were three desks, two of which had paper piles and manila folders stacked on top. There was a black pleather couch pushed against an adjacent wall with two accompanying chairs; in between was a small glass coffee table with tossed about copies of Penthouse and A.V.N. magazine. And lounging across the couch was the man himself, wearing a ruffled button down, a loose black tie, sunglasses, and he was sipping an energy drink.

"Ladies and gentlemen," he announced, "it's Logan Pierce."

"At your service," I said.

Lifting his sunglasses, Max studied me, his bloodshot eyes scanning from my shoes to my hair. "Hm," he said. "Kinda figured you'd be taller."

"Is that a problem?" I said, his eyes still lingering,

"...Nah; its all the same laying down, right?" He lowered his sunglasses and gulped the remainder of the can. Crushing the aluminum, he pointed to one of the chairs and said, "Sit down, kid, let's go over some brass tacks."

I sat and listened.

"Look, I want to make this very clear," He began. "It's nothing personal, mind you, but I don't exactly have a ton of faith in your ability, and before you say anything, just know that I get hundreds of guys coming to me asking to get them work, and I do because I like money, but very rarely, VERY rarely, are you guys actually capable of doing the job. Trust me, it all looks so easy when you're at home jacking off in front of your computer, but once you step foot on set, it's a whole new devil, you got it?

"Uh...yes sir."

"Great. Okay, now some tricks of the trade. Do not, under any circumstances, jerk off or have sex the morning of your scene; it sounds stupid, but trust me, a lot of guys make this mistake and fuck themselves over. I don't know why they do it, but it happens. Also, you got a girlfriend?"

"Mhm," I said, nodding.

"Might want to take care of that," he said, callously.

"Just saying, *civilians* often get in the way."

"Civilians?" I asked.

"If they're not in the business, they're on the outside," he said. "Civilians. Also, don't get any fucking tattoos; they'll make you instantly recognizable, and nobody wants to recognize one of the dudes; it takes away your, what do they call it—*anonimousness.*"

"…Anonymity," I said.

"Yeah, Exactly, that's what I said, kid. Oh, and the most important tip I can give you, is always, always, *always* open up the penetration to the camera, because if the cameras can't see the *Penny*, all the audience gets is man-blanket, and at that point you might as well be shooting gay soft-core, understand?"

"Always open up. Got it."

Max stood and showed me the door. "Now get outta here and head over to *Talent HQ* in Northridge to get yourself tested. They'll be expecting you."

"Sure," I said, "no problem."

He patted me on the back. "Don't worry," he said. "You're gonna do fine, Kid."

"Thank you, Max."

"Rock and Roll."

I drove to another part of the Valley and into yet another strip mall. Once again there were no signs, but on the front door was a small golden plaque bearing the name of the office.

Talent HQ, as I learned, is the industry sanctioned testing facility. In order to be eligible to perform on screen, all talent must first test negative for HIV, Chlamydia, Gonorrhea, and Syphilis; the basic panel, as it's referred to. It cost $165 and is a bi-weekly requirement.

I walked into Talent HQ and into a small waiting room. Approaching the reception desk, I gave the woman my name.

"Max from Sky Models sent me over," I said.

Checking a clipboard, she said, "Ah yes, Mr. Pierce." I gave her my debit card as she reached into a drawer and handed me a small plastic cup. "Fill this please." She directed me to the bathroom. I filled it and returned, placing the cup on a tray next to half a dozen other pee-filled cups. "Follow me," she said, leading me into a small backroom that I assumed must've been a storage closet before becoming a makeshift blood-drawing station. There was one chair and next to it was a vertical stack of shelves that were definitely bought on-sale at *Target*. They were stocked with pre-packed alcohol swabs, butterfly needles, and test tubes. She sat me down, wiped the crease of my elbow with a swap, and tied a tourniquet around my bicep. She handed me a boob shaped stress reliever and unwrapped a butterfly needle, attaching one end of it to a test tube. She stuck me and I watched intently as my blood coiled through the small rubber straw and into the plastic vial. She removed the needle, tossed it in a red biohazard container, and wrapped my arm in a cloth tape bandage.

I left Talent HQ and was finally on my way to the Oakwoods, ready to check in and knock out. I got my key, navigated through the maze of hallways, and found the door to room U-114. I half expected to find a glorified dorm with cots and a mini-fridge, but was more than surprised to find the room fully furnished with two couches, a dining table, a TV, and a full set of dishes and silverware in the kitchen. Not bad at all.

The bedroom, however, left a lot to be desired. In it were three twins sized beds, placed side-by-side in a line down the wall like kids at camp. I figured my roommates must've already been here because two of the beds—the two end beds—already had luggage on them, leaving me with no other choice but the one in the middle. I tossed my bags and walked into the bathroom to take a long shower.

While toweling off, I admired myself in the mirror. I had finally made it, I thought. The gears were greased and soon they would be turning; the plan was in motion. A pivotal speech from one of my all-time favorite movies came to mind, and I laughed at the thought of me repeating it to my reflection. Instead, I pointed at myself and mimicked the main character, singing, "You got the touch!" I slung the towel over my shoulder and strutted out the door, naked and still singing, "You got the Power!" I mock-karate kicked past the opening to the living room to discover my new roommates, who were once sitting on the couch breaking up weed on top of the coffee table, but were now writhing like banshees.

In a flash, I yanked down the towel and wrapped it around myself. "Holy shit!" I yelled, utterly embarrassed, running to the bedroom. I unpacked a pair of gym shorts and a t-shirt, threw them on, and walked back into the living room. Making the best of it, I said, "Well that's one way to make a first impression."

The bigger of the two, a dark Italian guy with a mop of shaggy black hair said, "Something tells me we're gonna get to know each other pretty closely over the next couple months."

"You got that right," added the skinnier, paler one with wire framed glasses and a backwards Phillies Cap, "That bed situation is a joke."

Shaggy hair perked up and said, "But fuck it; we're in LA, baby!" he extended his hand to me. "What's up, man? My name's Bernie."

I shook it. "Bernie, good to meet you. Without doubt you are definitely the first Bernie I've ever met."

"It's a *power* name," he said. "It's coming back, you'll see."

The bookish one brushed weed debris off of his fingers and stuck out his hand. "I'm Lou," he said.

"Bernie and Lou; I love it."

Scanning the coffee table, I noticed there were large multicolored pill bottles, a small tin bucket, and the top half of a two-liter soda bottle. "So, what kind of science experiment do you guys have going on here?"

"We're making a gravity bong," said Bernie.

"The good old G.B.," said Lou. "See, we'll take the tin, fill it up with water, then stick in the top half of the bottle, which I will outfit with a special cap I had fused with the bowl from my old bong; it's real MacGyver shit we're doing."

"I dig it," I said, "and what's up with the pill bottles?"

"Bro," Bernie said, "the weed came in them, isn't that nuts? I've never seen anything like it before. I am so used to buying baggies—"

"Or in like some plastic wrap that someone burnt shut with a lighter," added Lou.

"Times are tough on the east coast," I said. "So, how long have you two known each other?"

"For like that past two hours," said Bernie.

"Yeah," said Lou. "He also danced into the room dick swinging."

"Oh, fuck off," I said, playfully.

"Fellas," Bernie said. "The weed is ground. Lets spark this thing; I want to be thoroughly stoned before orientation tonight."

"Incontestably," said Lou.

"Yes," I said. "Indubitably so."

We filled the tin, secured the lid, and lit the bowl. Over the next half hour, I learned that Bernie was an aspiring writer, who, on any given day, carries three notebooks of varying sizes and purposes. And Lou was a cinematographer, his DSLR always on-hand, ready to capture the moment. Like me, they were both out here to chase the dream. Even half-past ripped; I could already tell the three of us were going to be friends. Still, I postponed sharing my little secret, for now, at least.

"So, Lou," I said, "what do you usually like to shoot with?"

"Well, right now," he said, brandishing his camera. "I use is this Lumix because it shoots 4K, and it's super low-profile. But, ideally, I'd want to shoot everything with the Alexa, probably with some Arri Master Primes, Panavision Primos, or maybe some cool vintage anamorphics, you know?"

"…Totally," I said, staring expressionless, the technical specs having gone way over my head.

"What can I say?" said Lou, "I have expensive tastes."

Changing topics I said, "All right, Bernie, inquiring minds want to know, what is the story with your notebooks?

"Its a three-act play," he said, grabbing his notebooks and presiding in front of the TV. Showcasing a large pad, he said, "Act one: the sketch pad for my drawings." He tossed the pad aside and grabbed a black and white notebook. "Act two: the composition book. This is *obviously* my journal." He tossed it and retrieved a small pocket-sized notebook from, where else, his back pocket. 'Act three: my book of finances."

"Isn't that what bank statements are for?" asked Lou, steaming from a fresh rip.

"Yeah, but I don't trust banks," he said. "Plus, it's more fun this way. I even use a specific color for that one: red, naturally."

"Naturally," I said.

Bernie tossed his notebooks aside and returned to the couch. "Time me," he said before taking another pull of the gravity bong. When his lungs were sufficiently filled, he held his breath.

I counted, "One, two, three—." Bernie burst out a thick cloud of white smoke; hacking so hard he had to take a knee to recover.

Disoriented, he said, "Whoa, I am fucking stoned, dog. *Stony-Bologna.*"

And with that, it was time for us to go to class.

12

I woke bright and early, Bernie and Lou fast asleep on either side of me. I stumbled into the living room, stretched, and did fifty pushups. I showered, brushed my teeth, and grabbed my suitcase and garment bag, leaving room U-114 and heading toward the parking garage. I drove thirty minutes west on the 101, through the valley and into the canyons of Calabasas, pulling up to a house in the middle of an affluent cul-de-sac, the neighbors blissfully unaware of my intention to go inside and fuck a stranger on camera for money.

This is it; don't get scared now.

I took a deep breath, shut off my car, grabbed my clothes, and walked toward the house, ready to work. I knocked on the front door, and a dark figure loomed through the opaque glass. The door opened and standing there was a six-foot tall, three hundred pound Samoan man dressed in a baggy tracksuit, sunglasses, and flip-flops. His lips parted and he cracked a smile, exposing titanium wires and bracket-covered teeth.

"*Logan Pierce?*" he said, sticking out his right hand.

"Name's *Duke*."

"Nice to meet you, Duke," I said, shaking his hand.

"You're a lot shorter than I imagined."

"Story of my life."

Duke led me to the dining room where I set down my stuff. The makeup artist was at the table, packing up her kits, filing away brushes, concealers, and endless varieties of eye shadow.

"She's all yours," she said, snapping shut her final case.

"Thanks Charlene," said Duke. "I got a check for you right here."

He walked her to the door, leaving me alone. I wandered into the kitchen and found my co-star. She was wearing white *Chuck Taylors*, knee high tube socks, frayed daisy-dukes, and a knotted flannel. Her skin was a creamy white and her strawberry blonde hair was done up in pigtails. She was arching against the marble counter-tops, idling on her phone.

She looked up. "Oh, hi!" she said, surprised. "Sorry, I didn't see you there, sometimes I just get so sucked into this thing."

"No problem," I said. "I was kind of in shock, myself. You look like a dream."

"Awe that's so sweet," she said.

I stuck out my hand, saying out loud for the very first time, "Hi, my name's Logan."

She came in for a hug. "Hi, I'm Carly," she said.

"Well, Carly," I said, my arm still around her, "looks like we'll be working together today."

"Partners in crime," she said.

Duke approached, patting me on the back. "Damn, she's a piece, huh?" he said. "You're a lucky motherfucker today."

Just then, as if on cue, Carly's phone slipped out of her hand and onto the floor, and as she bent at the waist to pick it up, I admired the way her outfit accentuated her body and hugged her curves with great fluidity.

"...Yes I am," I said.

"Alright Kids," said Duke. "What do you say we make some porno magic, huh?"

Carly and I were playing a young couple in the early stages of their budding romance. We were given a small Sony handy-cam and free reign of the house to shoot fifteen minutes of "storyline" footage, all from my P.O.V. Things like, flirting at the breakfast nook, me massaging Carly's feet on the couch, and us getting a little grabby in the laundry room. Then things heat up with a provocative strip tease. Lips moisten, veins throb, and Bam! An impromptu sex-tape begins.

Carly blew me at the base of the stairs, playing up the plot to the camera. "Oh my God, babe, I can't believe I'm letting you film this," she said. "It better not end up on the internet."

"Don't worry", I said. "It's just for us to see,"

"The camera actually turns me on," she said. "Lets do something crazy."

"Like what?" I asked.

"Let's go outside," she said, pulling me by my cock to the patio where we fucked poolside on a lounge chair, first doggy style and then cowgirl.

It was textbook porn; everything I had come to know and revere. And it was all so perfect, even with Duke lurching over my shoulder, breathing down my neck the entire time as he monitored the action to guarantee clear shots of the *penny*. I guess I should have found that a bit strange; most people would probably find it, at the very least, distracting, but not me. Having a voyeur actually turned me on, made me feel coveted. I was firing on all cylinders, proving my worth, and showcasing my talent.

We went back inside and set the camera on a tripod, allowing Carly and I the freedom to actually interact as two whole people. Time to introduce a face to match the cock.

And it was here I became a bit too eager and made a rookie mistake. Lost in the thrill, I was caught off guard by an unexpected and over-stimulating rush of joy. Realizing my doom all too late, I pulled out of Carly at critical mass and clamped myself with every ounce of strength I had.

Through white knuckles and grit teeth, I pleaded, "No, please no," but it was futile; ropes of shame shot all over Carly's pelvis and thighs.

"Are you fucking serious?" Duke wailed. "The *pop* was supposed to be a facial!"

"I'm sorry," I said through labored breaths. "I didn't mean to."

"Unbelievable," Duke scoffed, taking out his cellphone and furiously swiping his thumb across the screen while muttering to himself.

There was a brief moment of panic. In porn, the pop-shot is paramount. It serves as the most effective exclamation mark to everything that led up that point. My involvement with this production wasn't just about my pleasure; it was about working with a team to create a product. It was about doing a job, and right now, if I didn't get it back together, that relationship would be compromised.

Doe-eyed, I looked at Carly. She smiled and peered toward her now glistening skin. "Big load," she cooed, dipping two fingers into the sticky mess and lapping them clean. "Tastes good too." She licked her lips and reached out for my cock, petting it. "It's so perfect," she said. "Please, can I keep playing with it?"

She knew exactly what to say because suddenly I didn't feel so bad anymore. I regained my edge.

Channeling Dirk Diggler, I crowed, "I can do it again!"

Looking up from his phone, Duke saw my hard-on and grinned a mouthful of metal. "Music to my fucking ears," he said. "Let's do it."

We carried on and soon my very first porno came to its rightful and intended conclusion.

Cut. Print.

As we got dressed, Carly asked me to take a picture of her flashing her tits. I used my phone, and afterward she took it and put her number in, saving the photo as her caller ID.

"In case you want to get together sometime," she said, hugging me and sneaking a kiss on my cheek.

Duke walked over; check in hand. "Not bad for a first timer," he said. "I'll definitely have some more gigs for you in the future."

"Thanks, man. I appreciate that."

I shook his hand goodbye and hopped in my car, calling Allie to tell her the good news.

"It was crazy!" I said. "We fucked all over the house. She even made me cum twice, I couldn't believe—"

"That's okay," she said, cutting me off. "You don't have to tell me all the details."

"Oh…I'm sorry," I said.

"No, don't be," she said, "but you don't have to tell me everything you did."

"I just thought you would get a kick out of it," I said.

"I do. I'm happy for you, and I'm glad you had a good day," she said.

There was awkward silence. "Well, how was your day?" I asked.

"Eh, same old," she said. "Work and school."

My phone beeped; it was Max.

"Hey, is it okay if I call you back later?" I asked, "Someone's on my other line."

"Yeah, sure," she said. "I'm about to head to the restaurant anyway."

"Okay. I'll talk to you later," I said. "I love you."

"Love you too," she said, hanging up.

I answered Max's call.

"Hey Kid," he said. "Just talked to Duke. He says you popped twice; says you're the real deal. So what do you think, you want a couple more of these?"

"Hell yeah I do."

"How's Thursday and Friday? One Boy/Girl a piece. Four-hundred per."

"Fucking awesome," I said.

"Let's get you in the office this week so we can take some profile shots for the website."

"Sure. Thank you, Max."

"No problem. Keep it up, kid. Rock and Roll."

Back at the Oakwoods, high on life and Green Crack, I broke the news to the guys.

"Get the fuck out of here," Bernie said, "You? YOU!?" I don't believe it."

"Got any proof?" Lou asked.

"Actually," I said, reaching for my phone, "I have a picture of my *co-star*." I showed them the photo of Carly. They were beside themselves.

"Fuck me, she's a ten," Bernie said.

"So should we start calling you Chest Rockwell now or what?" Lou joked.

"No," I said. "But you can call me Logan Pierce."

"Logan Pierce? That name is sick," Lou said, throwing his arm around me. "Can you believe it? "Our own roommate: a fucking porn star. So, what did they shoot it with?"

"Used a Handy-cam today," I said, miming a camera aimed at my crotch. "P.O.V. Style."

"Classic," he said.

"You?" Bernie continued, incredulous, "YOU!?"

'

13

On Thursday, I was booked for a scene with the company *Evil Angel*. This was a stroke of luck for me. I had been jacking off to Evil Angel's content for years now; its name is synonymous with wholesome, quality smut. So, needless to say, I wanted to make a solid first impression.

The theme of the day was pseudo incest, or, "faux-cest," as it's called in the business. Since the inception of porn, audiences have been captivated by the idea of stepfathers deflowering their stepdaughters, or stepsiblings succumbing to impure urges; they love it when sex is kept in the family, and why shouldn't they? It's dark, its taboo, and its evil.

My co-star was a "M.I.L.F" performer by the name of *Nina Knives*. With big fake tits, luscious lips, gaudy nails, and a head full of platinum blonde extensions, Nina was the archetypal whore, and she was exactly my type. I played Nina's stepson—a rich and spoiled snob with a wanton desire for his stepmother the whore.

On camera, I lurked and spied as Nina sunbathed by the pool, sneaking up behind her, and taking a savoring whiff of her hair and perfume.

"Can I help you with something?" she asked.

"Oh no," I said. "I'm just enjoying the sites...and the smells."

Puzzled, Nina grabbed her things and walked back into the house. I scurried behind, following her upstairs into the master bathroom. With the door ajar, I watched as she stripped naked in front the mirror before stepping into the shower. That's when I made my move. I flung open the shower door and joined her fully dressed under the running water.

"What the hell are you doing?" she said as I lunged at her, my prying hands surveying every inch of her body. I grabbed the back of her head and pulled her close.

"If you don't like it, stop me," I said, pressing our lips together, my tongue rooting down her throat.

Nina's tense body relaxed, and she soon gave in to temptation. Pulling away, she confessed, "I've wanted this since the moment your father introduced us. But he can never know about this. It's our secret."

"Our *dirty* little secret," I said.

Nina tore down my pants, and we fucked under the steamy water, my clothes soaking to my skin and her eyeliner streaming in a gloriously gothic fashion.

Thirty minutes later, I gave Nina a pearl necklace and the director enthusiastically yelled, "Cut! Fucking great, guys. I loved it."

"Goddamn, Mr. Pierce," said Nina. "That was a hell of a scene. You better stick around, we need more guys like you."

"Thanks, Nina. I'll play your step-son any day."

We cleaned up; I got my check and hit the road.

Max called.

"That's twice now," I said. "How do you know the exact moment I leave set?"

"I got eyes everywhere, kid. So, listen, tomorrow's cancelled."

"Shit. It wasn't because of me or anything, was it?"

"No, no. Scenes get cancelled all the time, it's nothing, they lost the girl, so it's not happening anymore, however, I got something else for you, could be something big."

"Really?"

"It's an interview with *Provocateur X*."

Provocateur X was a new studio that specialized in producing *Glamcore*, a style of porn for the romantic masturbator. Glamcore is soft and intimate; foreplay is paramount, and the most commonly uttered phrase on set is, "Make love, not porn."

The next morning, I went to meet with the in-house director, *Bo Berry*, at the Provocateur X studios in Culver City. When I arrived, Bo was in another meeting, so his assistant led me to his office. While waiting I noticed one of a few framed diplomas hanging above his desk was from Temple University.

"Small fucking world," I said, the door opening behind me.

"You can say that again," Bo said, entering with a brisk trot. "It is I, I am he; Bo Berry, pleasure to meet ya."

"Nice to meet you too," I said, noticing a half smoked joint tucked behind his ear. "I'm actually a Temple student myself."

"Well, what do you know about that? It's always good to meet a fellow owl."

"So, when did you graduate?" I asked.

Regarding the diploma, he said, "Well let's see, it all started back in the year 1796 on a farm in—No, I'm only kidding. Oy, I was a different man back then, but I was class of 1999. Yes, that's where I got my undergrad before getting the hell away and moving on to bigger and better things." He pointed to another diploma, this one from AFI—the most prestigious film school in the country.

"Like, *the* AFI?" I asked.

"That's the one," he said.

"Fuck off," I said, joking.

"Hey, now you're starting to sound like my ex-wife," he said. "Oy gevalt! But, enough of the past; let's discuss the future." Bo paced the room. "Did your agent tell you what I wanted to do?" I opened my mouth to speak, but the question was rhetorical. "No, of course they didn't," he said. "All they tell the talent is where to go and who to fuck, and lets be honest, they even screw that up sometimes. But this will be something important. This will be original. I want to create something raw, something organic, do you follow?"

"I think I have an idea," I said.

"I want this to be like the *first* time," he said. "And that's actually the title: 'My First Time.' Fucking genius, right?"

"So, you're saying you want the scene to last sixty seconds?" I said. "Because I can totally do that for you."

Without skipping a beat, Bo said, "Exactly. A totally experimental piece, blink and you miss it. It'll revolutionize the business." He took a deep breath, closed the distance between us, and lowered his tone. "But seriously, what do you think?"

"You want it to be real; no acting," I said.

"No porno talk," he said. *"Oh, rail my soaking wet pussy with your tube steak!* None of that crap."

"You want two people sharing a private moment," I said.

"I want two people in love," he countered.

"...In love," I repeated.

"That's right," he said. "Cameras are non-existent. Although, for you, personally, there'll be three cameras, a full grip team, the sound guy, two PA's, one line producer, and of course, me, scrutinizing your every move. But as far as the audience is concerned, you're all alone."

"...Right," I said.

"So," he said, searching for clues on my face. "What

do you think?"

"I dig it," I said. "Honestly, I was already on-board before you even walked through the door."

"Well, thanks for making me deliver the entire spiel," he said, removing the joint from his ear and putting it between his lips. "Now I still have a few faces to see, and I can't promise anything, but what do you say, you want to make a fucking movie?"

14

At night, the boys and I lounged in one of the Oakwood's oversized Jacuzzis, sipping beers and passing a bowl. My first week in California and I'd already become a stoner.

"Look at us," I said. "It's January, and we're chillin' in a hot-tub without a care in the world, while everyone back home is freezing their asses off."

"Better luck next time, suckers!" Bernie shouted into the ether.

"I have a great idea," said Lou, perking up. "You boys wanna hit the town?"

"What do you got in mind?" I asked.

"Oh, don't you worry your handsome little face," he said, rubbing his hands together as if he were plotting world domination. "Lets be ready to leave in forty-five. Tonight's dress code: Money, baby."

An hour later, we were dressed in dark suits and ties, on our way into Hollywood toward a newly opened speakeasy; it's entry: by reservation only.

Out front, the place was non-descript. No sign, no

line, just a door cast in neon red and a well-dressed doorman with a clipboard.

We approached and Lou took the lead. "We have a reservation for three," he said. "Under the name, *Vincenzo Espinosa*."

The doorman eyeballed us before checking his clipboard. He reported into his headset walkie-talkie, "I have three coming up," he said, stepping aside and granting us access.

We walked through the door and ascended a dark stairwell outlined with burning prayer candles.

"Espinosa's the boss at my internship," Lou said. "Guy's obsessed with this place; told me I could drop his name anytime."

The stairs led to a room resembling a shabby hotel lobby from the roaring twenties, prohibition signs tacked on the walls.

Stepping out from behind the would-be reception desk, a woman dressed as a provocative bellhop greeted us and set the guidelines. "No flash photography of the in-house band or the burlesque dancers, and the only exit is located on the ground floor, that is, once you go down you don't come back up, got it?"

"Got it," we said in unison.

She opened an adjacent armoire, and inside the double doors were velvet maroon curtains. She pulled them aside to uncover another passageway.

"Gentlemen, welcome to El Baile."

We walked through the darkness and onto a metal grate walkway; the sounds of live music reverberated off the floor and through the walls, swelling into a crescendo as more light was revealed. We reached a balcony overlooking a sea of opulent patrons sipping crafted cocktails and salsa dancing as an Afro-Cuban jazz band jammed from a stage below.

"Ay dios mio!" we cheered.

We went down a spiral staircase and hit the bar. Lou immediately sparked a conversation with a woman who was waiting for her date to arrive.

"Aw, come on, sweetheart, it's not like he's here right now," he coaxed.

"Yeah, no thanks, kid," she said, taking her drink elsewhere.

"Fuck it," he said, looking back at us. "I'm buying the first round." He slammed his palm on the bar and yelled, "Three Cuba Libres!"

"Hey, what a guy!" said Bernie, slapping Lou's shoulder.

I leaned against the bar and scanned the room. I spotted a gorgeous blonde just out of earshot, wearing a red cocktail dress and sipping wine while swinging her hips to the music.

The Woman in red.

She looked my way and our eyes locked, but I hesitated, sheepishly burying my face behind Bernie.

"Why don't you go talk to her?" he asked.

"Ah, I don't know," I said. "I hate having to come up with opening lines. Plus, I have a girlfriend."

"Sure, sure; hey, I got a girl back home too," he said. "But…it's not like you haven't already been banging other chicks."

"Yeah, but that's different; its for work."

"Work, Ha! That's rich," he said. "Okay, put it like this: nobody says you need to take her into the bathroom, but there's nothing wrong with a little flirtation, right?"

"Yeah, yeah," I said, looking back toward the woman in red as she chatted with a small group of girlfriends. I contemplated walking over, but instead I let the moment pass.

We finished our drinks and I bought the next round. We walked around the club, making our way into the back room—a dimly lit cigar lounge shrouded in thick clouds of tobacco. Stepping inside, we filled our lungs with the savoring scent.

"You guys thinking what I'm thinking?" Said Lou.

"Stogies!" we howled.

"I'm on it," said Bernie, already approaching the bar.

Five minutes later, we reclined on fashionably ripped leather seats with smoke billowing all around us.

"To the night!" we cheered, clinking glasses and gnawing cigar heads.

Suddenly, the woman in red returned. With two friends, she walked into the lounge and right back into my life; a second chance, I thought, but I was still at a loss.

Thankfully, Lou sprang into action and got their attention. Introductions were made all around and her and I casually gravitated toward one another.

I reached out my hand. "Hi, what's your name?"

Softly, almost inaudibly, she said something that sounded like, "Eye-wah."

"...I'm sorry?" I said, without a clue.

Louder, she said, "My name is Eira—E-I-R-A."

"Ohh, Eira," I said, having never heard a name like that before. "That's a new one, pretty neat."

"It's Welsh, "she said. "I'm from Sylvania."

"No shit?" I said. "Funny enough, I am from *Pennsylvania*. How interesting!"

"Yes, very," she said, obviously uninterested.

"...So, what brought you to Los Angeles?

"I'm visiting a friend in the states."

Again, misunderstanding her I said, "You're moving into your own place?"

"No," she said, sighing and then taking a deep breath. Speaking slowly, she reiterated, "I am visiting. You know: tourist!"

"Oh, cool. Sorry, it's pretty loud in here," I said. "So... Sylvania; that's where Dracula is from right?"

Looking around she said, "I don't think I know who that is."

"No?"

"No," she said. "Um, I'm going to talk to my friend for a minute."

"Oh, okay, cool."

She turned away, and I retreated to the bar.

Bernie joined me. "Hey, how did that go, stud?"

"I'm fucking blowing it," I said.

"Why don't you buy her a drink? It's a perfect ice-breaker."

"Yeah? Okay, wish me luck," I said, making a B-line toward her. I tapped her on the shoulder and hijacked her attention away from her friend. "Hey, how about I get you a drink?" I asked.

She looked at me and then to her friend and then back to me. "Sure," she said. "A glass of red?"

"Red wine. Easy. Be right back," I said.

Piece of cake. How could I possibly screw this up?

My first mistake was leaving her alone as I went to the bar. The minute I stepped away I saw another man swoop in; a man I recognized to be taller, better dressed, and better looking.

"Son of a bitch," I muttered to myself.

Then, caught up with the inconvenient arrival of the hunk, I blindly ordered "Sauvignon" from the bartender with a certain sense of assurance in my voice. In horror, I watched him pour a glass of white wine, and feeling too embarrassed to admit my mistake, I just paid for the drink and sulked back to Eira and her new date.

Regretfully, I handed her the glass and apologized that it was white, fabricating a story to make the bartender appear like the idiot. "I told him *Cabernet*; he must've gotten confused," I said. Eira smiled and nodded before turning back to the taller, more attractive bastard.

Defeated, I walked back over to Bernie.

"Wanna get out of here?" I asked. "Get some food?"

"Thinking Tacos?"

"Absolutely."

"Let's do it," he said, gulping the rest of his drink.

We grabbed Lou, and together the three of us exited the club and reentered the city streets, returning back into the wild in search of the nearest taco truck. Lucky for us, there's one on every corner in this town.

We wolfed down some carnitas and al-pastor and wandered around the block. I noticed an apartment complex with an accessible fire escape perfectly composed up the center of the building, something not too often seen in Los Angeles.

"Man, I never thought I'd miss seeing fire-escapes," I said.

"Yeah, there's something really cinematic about them," said Lou, framing the shot with his hands.

"Well," said Bernie, "What do you say?"

Lou and I looked at each other. Maybe it was the buzz of alcohol, the tobacco high, or just the spur of spontaneity, but without thinking twice, we started climbing.

At the top, we were rewarded with a panoramic view of the city. In front of us were Hollywood high-rises and the downtown skyline, and behind us the Church of Scientology buzzed as the Griffith Observatory hovered high above the masses.

"Damn. Can't beat rooftop views," said Bernie.

"It's really something else," I said.

"I couldn't imagine a more perfect setting," said Lou, taking out a joint from his suit pocket and lighting it. "Take it in, boys," he said. "Take it in."

My phone rang. It was Allie. Jesus, it must've been close to 3 a.m. back home. Maybe she was just calling to say goodnight, or maybe it was something more serious. I know I probably should've answered, but a part of me wanted to breath in the present just a little longer. I figured I'd call her back in the morning, pretend like I had been asleep, so I silenced the ring and ignored her.

The three of us stood near the edge and passed the joint, marveling at the harmonious chaos of the vibrant lights, and for a moment, life was tranquil, just a cool breeze on a private rooftop in Hollywood.

15

My internship started the following Monday. For the remainder of the semester, from 9-5, Monday-Wednesday, I would belong to Veneer Pictures.

Their offices were in Beverly Hills, right in the heart of 90210, wealth and opulence flaunted in the streets, restaurants, and boutique shops like its going out of style. And yet, I couldn't help but imagine if it was all just a grand illusion, some sort of a desperate reach for grace before the credit cards ran dry; almost as if to say, "But at least I was there before it all went to hell."

That, and the parking was shit.

My superior at Veneer was an NYU alumnus named Jonas, personal assistant to the V.P. of productions. He worked sixty hours a week for a meager paycheck and no benefits, besides the social variety, of course.

"I may not have health insurance," he said. "But I can get a same-day reservation at Nobu on a Saturday night if I use my boss' name. Not just anyone can do that, you know."

"Must be nice," I said, reeling in the weekend.

All day long Jonas sat at his desk answering the phones, mediating calls, and updating spreadsheets. In between, he remained glued to his computer screen—obsessively reading Deadline or The Hollywood Reporter, calculating box office takes and eating up industry gossip.

My office responsibilities included just about everything you would expect from a college intern; I made coffee, I made copies, I emptied the dishwasher, I organized storage closets, I picked up lunch, and I picked up laundry.

Working at Veneer solidified an innate, but as of yet, dormant, grudge I held toward the fluorescent light, headset, water-cooler bullshit. This was not where I saw myself, but for the time being I'd have to deal with it.

16

Friday morning, I arrived on set for Provocateur X. Home base was a cliff-side Malibu compound.

"Welcome to the Revolution," Bo said, coming out to meet me as I drove past the automated security gate. "I've always wanted to say that, but seriously, we're about to change the game. Mr. Pierce, how the hell are ya?"

"Feeling good, my friend."

"Glad to hear it, buddy. Park anywhere you want and come on in, we'll get you situated with paper work and all that."

Inside, the team was already hard at work, moving with unprecedented speed and efficiency. In total, there were twenty-five crewmembers—something practically unheard of in contemporary porn. Outside of the crew Bo had mentioned, there was a full catering team, two makeup artists, a designated hair stylist, and even nails for both the female and the male talent.

My co-star was a newcomer by the name of Paige Parker. Paige was nineteen, this was her first scene, and like me, she was full of wonder. This was a perfect opportunity for me to take the lead and play the nice guy, to make her feel comfortable and show her she has nothing to be nervous about as I hold her hand and shepherd her safely through the scene. The thought of that made me feel powerful.

The scene itself was a vignette chronicling two youngsters who are so madly in love that they run away to elope. And now, alone on their honeymoon, the only thing left to do is consummate. It was a virginal approach followed by a robust and passionate climax, and when the time came for me to do just that, Joe instructed me to "fuck-to-pop."

"Cake and pie," I said.

I worked until I felt the warmth, then I slipped out, and with a final thrust of my hips, I erupted, sowing the seeds of love all over Paige's tits and lower abdomen.

"Cut!" Bo roared. "Flawless, kids. Just flawless."

After getting my check, and while the crew was breaking down the set, I took a moment to myself on the back terrace. I sipped french pressed coffee and watched the sun set over the pacific shimmering blues spanning unto infinity.

Oh yeah, I definitely saw myself getting used to this.

17

Word was out; Logan Pierce is hot, he's fresh; he's the new boy next door. Max was calling me practically every day with scene offers, and before I knew it, I had twelve more days booked. I was starting to build a reputation, well on my way to becoming a *somebody*.

But back at Veneer, I was nothing more than just another cog in the machine, my talent being grossly underappreciated. I figured I already had my ticket out of that supposed 'real world,' so I did what any respectable young professional would do: I stopped showing up to the office, and I ignored Jonas' phone calls until he got the hint and gave up. It was a coward's exit, for sure, but it got the point across.

"Fuck em," said Bernie. "I wish I could just quit like that. And on my way out, I'd take a big shit right on top of the dickhead V.P.'s desk."

"Yeah, I'm like the office bitch," said Lou.

"Exactly!" I said. "And it wasn't like they were going to hire me; they're just getting free labor. I mean, what's the point of this? Aren't we supposed to find a job we like? I already found a job, and I fucking love it."

"I'll smoke to that," said Bernie, lighting a joint.

He passed it to me and after a deep inhale I asked, "So, what's the one thing you guys wanted to accomplish in LA?"

"Well I planned to start my first novel out here," said Bernie. "But I guess I've been a little distracted lately. What do you say, Lou?"

"Listen," Lou said, taking a hit, "all I know is, before I go back home I want to shoot a movie—*need* to shoot a movie; I'd be a fool not to."

"Got that right," I said.

"Well…" Bernie said, completing the rotation, "what are we waiting for?"

"…You guys wanna shoot something?" I said.

"Lets fucking go!" said Lou.

———————————————————

The film was entitled "Meridian." It explored the notion of man's instinctive need to escape the constructs of society and return back into nature. Bernie wrote it, Lou shot it, and I acted in it. We took advantage of our time and the distinct cinematic landscape of the city. Principal photography occurred on the shores of Zuma Beach, in the meditation circle at Runyon Canyon, the sand dunes of Death Valley, and in the tucked away cliffs of the Santa Monica Mountains.

It was a sweaty, sometimes bloody, and often treacherous shoot, but that's what kept us alive. It was us saying 'fuck the system and fuck the rules.' We didn't wait for someone to give us permission to shoot; we went out and made it ourselves because we could. *This* was freedom.

With our pooled assets, we became the triple threat: Lou was the eye, Bernie was the mind, and I—well, I was the cock, the smoking gun, the wildcard.

After a week of editing footage in our blacked out apartment, Meridian, in all of its 3-minute glory, was complete and ready for upload to YouTube.

We celebrated the release with orange chicken, pot stickers, and three six-packs of *Simpler Times* lager. We gorged the meat and guzzled the beer, lighting a freshly rolled joint as we cracked into the second six-pack.

"All right," I said. "What's the second thing you guys want to accomplish in LA?"

"Honestly," said Lou, taking a drag, "I want to get a fucking tattoo." He handed the joint to Bernie, who contemplated before taking a hit.

"A tattoo," he said. "That would be cool."

I'd always wanted a tattoo, and even though Max had warned against it, I couldn't think of a more appropriate way to symbolize a chapter in my life—in our lives. It was time for new prospects; there was greatness on the horizon. My destiny was in my hands; all it would take was one step.

"Lets do it," I said. "Tonight."

The three of us looked around the table. The feeling was mutual.

"I'm in," said Lou.

"Fuck it, me too," said Bernie.

"But what do we get?"

We split the final six-pack and brainstormed. Meridian, among other elements, portrayed a man climbing a mountain, and during the writing phase we learned that the universal symbol for a mountain is a simple triangle. A triangle; It's meaningful, it's inconspicuous; it's perfect. And what better place than the chest? The left pec, we agreed, right above the heart.

9:00 pm. We shuffled toward the door and outside into the street. We taxied to the Sunset strip with plenty of time to think and over think and ponder and get cold feet, but still, nobody backed out.

On the strip, we walked into the first shop we saw— the word *Tattoo* strewn in bright neon letters, and like gnats to the light we were lured in. As an Acapella group, we slid across the counter and told the artist, who introduced himself as Toby, exactly what we wanted in great detail.

"A triangle," said Lou

"Three straight lines?" Asked Toby.

"That's it," I said.

"And all three of you want the same thing?"

"Yessir," said Bernie.

"No problem," he said. "Shop minimum is $100 per

person."

Shit. I may have been a virgin in the world of tattoos, but a hundred bucks for three little lines? It sounded borderline ridiculous to me, but when I looked at my friends I saw fiery determination in their eyes.

"You take debit, right?" I said.

"Absolutely," said Toby, grinning ear to ear.

Bernie was first in the chair, on edge, his right foot tapping with anxiety. On contact, his grimace softened as he realized the needle didn't hurt nearly as bad as he thought it would. Literally thirty-seconds later he was done and it was Lou's turn in the hot seat. He breathed through his teeth and admitted it was actually more painful than he expected.

Then it was my turn. Upon penetration, the needle sent a dull but constant vibration through my body, teetering on the bounds of pleasure and pain. I found comfort in it; the thirty-seconds it took to apply wasn't enough. I knew this wouldn't be my last time under the gun.

Toby pointed us in the direction of the shop's full-length mirror. We flexed and admired our new ink in the reflection. These three lines permanently etched into our skin signified the bond between us, a simple representation of solidarity and kinship. We would never again be alone in this life, and every conflict we individually face would be conquered with the strength of three men. Much like our bodies, our lives had been forever changed.

The school semester ended one month later. I drove Bernie and Lou to the airport, giving them both a fond farewell as they prepared to fly back to Pennsylvania. The three of us made a pact to stay in touch.

"And don't forget," I said, "when you guys get tired of home, there's always a couch waiting for you back on the best coast."

"Thanks, kid," said Lou.

"Till the wheels come off," Said Bernie.

"See you soon, Guys."

For the rest of the students, it was time to leave, but I was just getting started. I lied to my parents and told them Veneer had asked me to stay and intern for the summer with the promise of full-time employment surely in the cards. They were ecstatic and encouraged me to stay and enjoy myself, but to be ready to come back and finish school in the fall.

I, of course, had other plans. I signed a one-year lease for an apartment in Tarzana, right off the 101, in the heart of Porno-land: my new home. This is where I belonged.

18

As promised, I flew Allie out to visit. We spent our mornings hiking, our afternoons at the beach, and our nights at dinner and the movies. We carried on like kids in love.

During her stay, I was invited as a special guest for a radio show called *Probing the Industry*. It was hosted by a flamboyant ex-performer named *Roy Genoa*, and staying true to his name, Roy looked as if he ate a few too many hoagies in the past. Nowadays, Roy mainly worked as the porno equivalent to a character actor, appearing in "non-sex" rolls, as they're referred to. He was proud of his show, always raving about his frequency of broadcasts and his "millions" of listeners. I figured my appearance would be good press and a great way to introduce my civilian girlfriend to the industry.

In the car on our way to the studio, I prepped Allie for what she might expect.

"Just be warned," I said. "People in this business tend to be a bit more, uh, *forward*."

"Hands on? Like groping and stuff?" she asked.

"No, no, not like that," I said. "Just, Roy might hug

you a little too long or compliment you on your body or say weird, kind of creepy things—but I promise it's all in good fun."

"Fun," she said, tense at the thought.

We arrived at 6:45 and took an elevator from the parking garage up to the studio. When we entered, Roy was already in the booth, on the air, and with a naked girl sitting in his lap. Across from them sat another girl, also naked, attempting to fit a soda can into her mouth as Roy cheered her on.

I tried to signal him through the glass window, but he waved me away, putting up his index finger as if to say, "Wait a minute."

So we did. We sat outside the booth for nearly fifteen minutes before Roy opened the door to let us in.

"Oh, boy, another plaything," he said, scanning Allie before returning to his seat. He patted his knee, and said, "Come sit on daddy's lap."

Allie threw me a look of disdain. "No, thanks," she said. "I'll stand."

"Meow," Roy said, miming a cat's claw. "You gotta sharp one here, Pierce."

"Fitting, isn't it?" I said, sitting across from Roy in the only available seat, in-between the two naked girls from before, who were now wearing silk robes.

"Ladies," Roy said, "say hello to Logan. He's the new *stud* on the block."

The one to my left, dark skin with pink hair and a septum piercing, draped her right leg over my knee. "Hi new stud," she said.

The other, middle aged with fading tattoos, let her robe fall; she had a fresh boob job and was eager to show off the new hardware. "Cougar snack," she purred, grazing my shoulder with her long acrylic nails.

"Hi ladies," I said, modestly.

I looked at Allie and shrugged my shoulders, as if to say, *see; it's not so bad.* Her stare said she disagreed. She scoffed, kneeling on the floor and pulling out her phone to distract herself, to distance herself.

"Okay, so this is how it'll work," Roy said. "We are back in a minute and when we go on the air I'm going to finish chatting with the girls. Then I'll introduce you and ask you a couple questions. That's it."

"That's it?"

"Yup."

"But, I thought—"

"Hush, hush," he said. "We're back in 5...4...3...2." He pushed a button, the on-air sign beamed red, and we were now live. I put on my headphones and listened in.

Roy lowered his voice to bedroom volume and said, "Hello, Hello, and welcome back all of you fellow perverts and *pervettes.* This is the human foot long himself, Dr. Genoa, here with my analysis. Speaking of anal, I am once again joined by my two stunning co-stars, *Tammy Cumz* and *Jade Jackson.*

Ladies, please say something for your adoring audience."

"Oh, god, I'm so wet," said the punk princess.

"I'm ready for sucky-fucky," said the M.I.L.F.

"And that's what I love about you, Tammy. You're always revved up, like a little *Energizer* sex-bunny."

"Oh, daddy," said Jade. "All of this talk about sex is getting me excited. What do you say, should I just start sucking his dick right now?"

Meaning me, Roy said, "The *dick* in question belongs to none other than new male talent, Logan Pierce. Logan, what do you think? Wanna whip it out right here in the studio?"

"You know me," I said. "I'm always up for it."

Allie jerked her head in my direction, her eyes burning a hole right through me.

"Maybe one day we'll book a scene together," I said, hoping to move on.

"You heard it here first, folks. Producers, get these kids together now. All right, lets return to our discussion. Logan, tell the audience, have you ever harbored any naughty feelings for a family member?"

"What!?" I shrieked, taken aback.

"Maybe diddle a cousin?" Roy asked. "The topic of the night is incest."

"Yeah," Tammy added. "I had a crush on my step-brother and even gave him a hand job when I was fourteen."

"You don't say?" I said, and then leaning into the

microphone, I added, "Um...to answer your question, Roy, no I didn't."

He pushed a button and a buzzer went off. "Boo! Boring!" he yelled. He reached under the table and pulled out a bottle of vodka. "You know what that means, everybody."

The girls chanted into their microphones, "Shots! Shots! Shots!"

Roy took a swig of the bottle and handed it to Allie, who promptly refused to drink. Then he handed it to me. Truth be told, I can't stand the taste of vodka, but I wanted to be a good sport, so I grabbed the bottle and took a shot. My eyes started to water as I fought to swallow.

Through my peripherals, I could see Allie covering her mouth as she laughed; it served me right.

"Aw, poor baby," Jade said, taking the bottle and a swig.

She handed it to Tammy, who took an extended gulp, theatrically spilling liquor down her chin and onto her chest. "Whoopsie," she said, licking her lips.

"Okay," Roy said into the mic. "Be sure to join us tomorrow night as we probe deeper and deeper and *deeper* into the industry. Goodnight, everyone." He pushed another button and the on-air sign went out. The show was over.

"Wow, that was great," Roy said. "Fantastic work, everybody." He stood and walked over to me, sticking out his hand. "Come back anytime, kid."

We shook. "Uh, yeah, sure," I said. "Thanks for

having me."

Roy turned his attention to his girls, who had resumed drinking from the bottle. "So, my little troublemakers," He said. "Where shall we eat? Daddy's starving."

Allie and I left the studio and took the elevator back down to the parking garage. The tension was palpable. In the car, I tried to break the silence.

"Look, uh…I'm sorry if that was uncomfortable."

"I don't want to talk about it," she said.

"It was kind of weird for me too," I said, trying to ignore the fact that if she hadn't been there, I probably wouldn't have thought twice about getting blown on live radio. "Fuck that guy," I said, looking for common ground.

"Can we just go home, please?" She asked.

"Yes," I said. "I'm sorry."

We went to bed without speaking. In the middle of the night we both stirred, sleepy eyed, and longing for affection. We kissed, and I pulled down my shorts and peeled her panties aside.

I shuffled on the bed and eagerly went down on her, pinning her legs in the air, keeping my face turned out, opening up the action like I would for the camera, performing my duty, doing my job.

Suddenly, I heard whimpering and looked up to see Allie with her hand over her mouth, fighting back tears. The moment was lost. Allie closed her legs and turned away, embarrassed, ashamed. I lay behind her, quietly holding her, unsure of what else to do.

As she cried in my arms she confessed, "I can't get the thought of that creep out of my mind. He was disgusting. Is that really what you want to become?"

"Baby, that's nothing like me," I assured.

"Oh my god. And incest—are you kidding me? I wanted to throw up."

"I promise I will never be like that," I said.

"It doesn't even matter," she said. Those are the people you work with, that's the company you're in." She started bawling. "This is wrong, okay? I don't…feel right. I feel used, like you're doing to me exactly what you would have done to those random girls tonight. Like there's no longer anything special or sacred about our sex."

I didn't have anything to say to convince her otherwise. I should have expected this. "It's not cheating, its work." Total bullshit, a fabrication repeated in my mind for a false sense of security. Of course it was cheating, I'd been fucking other people for money. A relationship like that can't survive; that's no way to treat someone I claimed to love.

I was reminded of an old song about a woman who falls in love with a man, but over time and countless arguments, she realizes she has not been herself, and that she changed who she once was to satisfy the needs of another. She was living a lie.

I wondered if I was turning Allie into something she didn't want to be, and if I was becoming someone she couldn't love anymore, someone unhealthy, someone bad. If I truly loved her I would've left now before I sank too deep. Then again, if I cared at all I wouldn't have exposed her in the first place. But I did. I ruined what we had, and now I would have to let her go.

WORKING STIFF

01

A typical working day for me begins at 8 a.m. I roll out of bed and do a short workout—100 pushups and 30 pull-ups. I shower, get dressed, and make a pot of coffee, skipping a big breakfast in favor of something light like a cup of fruit, a piece of toast, or a small bowl of cottage cheese. I double check my work bag and make sure it's packed with at least two pairs of shoes, two pairs of underwear, one pair of socks, three pairs of pants, two different belts, four or five varying t-shirts, my toiletry bag, my pills, my headphones, and a book. I then grab my ironed dress shirts and hit the road.

After anywhere between fifteen minutes and an hour I arrive at whatever address Max had given me the night before. Initially, I thought it was strange and almost inconsiderate of him to send me information that late, but I soon found out that most producers don't even know what they're shooting until the day before. "That's just how porn works," he told me.

I enter the house or studio and wander the halls, following the growing noise of chatter most likely coming from the "green room," which is, more often that not, doubling as the makeup studio.

My co-star is usually sitting in the makeup chair when I arrive. I'm affable and will introduce myself, (assuming we haven't already met) but other than that I'll wait to have a full conversation.

In the meantime, I fill out paperwork: a model release, condom waiver, blood born pathogen waiver, and a W-9. Then I read my book and kill time on my phone, listening to music or scrolling through Twitter. Much like any job in film production, the general motto is, "Hurry up and wait," and that's exactly what I do. I don't really mind, though. In fact, I tend to do a lot of quality reading while loafing around on set. I suppose there are worse ways for me to spend my time.

When my co-star is out of makeup, we chat. I'll try to make a few jokes to get her to laugh and feel comfortable; I learned that appealing to a stranger's sense of humor is a great way to charm them into having sex with me—that, and a decent paycheck, of course. We talk about nothing in particular: people we know in the business, companies we've shot for, the outdated décor of the house or the *Whore-ifficly* bare set design of the studio. If there's a script, we go over lines, but most of the time dialogue is improvised

Eventually, the director gathers us and takes *bunny-ear* shots of us individually holding our two required forms of ID—social security and driver's license—up to either side of our faces. I always give an exaggerated smile.

The director picks out my co-star's wardrobe from one

of her bloated suitcases, which overflow with bags of lingerie, stripper heels, cocktail dresses, sporty wear, professional wear, sex toys, and sometimes, on those rare occasions, a book. The director then asks me to wear something complimentary.

As a group we go over the proposed plan of attack. It's all the same, really; the couple will enter frame left and bullshit about who loves who, who's related to who, (with strong emphasis on the "step" prefix) who's cheating on who, etc. Then sex will invariably ensue.

We shoot stills before video because it serves as a template for the real thing. We mime the action corresponding with the "plot." Things like, "I can't do this, I'm married, and you're my wife's best friend!" We take two-dozen or so shots of each sex position: blowjob, pussy eating, missionary, cowgirl, doggie, reverse cowgirl, and finally, the pop-shot—which is *always* faked for stills with *Cetaphil* face wash applied vigorously to my co-stars face and tits.

After stills, we clean up, get dressed, and prepare to do everything all over again for video, and while mostly pre-determined, video is still actually very much free form. As long as we can effectively get from point A to point B with so much as a glimmer of grace, we are pretty much left to our own devices.

Naked, on display, and left at our most primal, our actions are no longer intellectual, rather, they've become visceral, fueled by pure adrenaline. We communicate exclusively through body language, feeding off of each other's energy. When executed properly, performing can be a boundless and animalistic form of uncensored self-expression.

After the pop, I grab baby wipes for my co-star and some for myself. I get dressed, get my paycheck, and say my goodbyes. At home, I reheat my morning pot of coffee and smoke a joint. Then I jack off again before taking a shower.

All in all, it's not such a bad gig.

02

It was the first day of summer. I showed up to set to find Chester Bang waiting for me, practically pissing his pants at my arrival.

"Broseph!" he said, throwing his arms around me. "Welcome to the family."

"Thanks, man," I said. "It's good to finally meet you. So, what, are you shooting a scene today too?"

"Nah, I'm the P.A.," he said. In other words, he's the guy who disinfects the couches and picks up the used baby wipes. "I don't mind, really, I just like being involved." Motioning toward two *Kino-flo* light kits he said, "I even donated my lights; I'm the best P.A. in the biz."

I found the director pacing by himself. He said my co-star was thirty minutes late. "And she's supposed to arrive make-up ready," he said. His phone rang. "Oh fuck, it's her agent." He ducked into the kitchen to take the call.

I lounged on the sofa and read *The Basketball Diaries* while Chester sat on an apple-box scrolling through Twitter, his free hand resting on his belly underneath his shirt.

Despondent, the director trudged back into the living room. Rubbing his stubbled chin, he said, "All right, here's the deal; just got off with her agent, and he says she popped a dirty test."

"Oh, gross, what'd she catch?" asked Chester, eager for the gory details.

"I don't know and I don't want to fucking deal with it," he said. "Pack up, guys. I'm calling it a day."

"Aw man," I grumbled, creasing my page and lazily grabbing my bag. On the surface, I was pissed—*Great, I drove all the way here for nothing*—but on the inside, I was secretly celebrating, overjoyed, even, by the flaking of my co-star. That's because the title of today's movie was, "She's Gotta Lotta Hair Down There #10."

I'll admit I'm not the biggest fan of the bush. That doesn't mean I want a woman completely smooth like plastic, it just means I prefer someone who is both trim and proper. When hair is running amok along the inner thighs, or crowding the lips, it's game over, man.

And it was my own stupid fault for taking the gig in the first place. All Max had said was that a particular company wanted to book me on a particular day for a particular fee. He sent my call-time the night before, and that was the extent of it. I didn't do my homework, and was subsequently sandbagged when I got to set.

So, when I heard the news, I was relieved.

"I guess I'm already in the valley," I said. "Might as

well go get tested myself."

Chester perked up. "Oh, me too," he said. "Testing HQ?"

"Testing HQ," I said.

"Hash-tag Team Northridge!" he said.

"Ha, absolutely."

"Well if you're already headed there," he said, "Can I just ride with you? Otherwise I have to catch a bus—well, two busses, actually, and I have my gear with me and these cases are like fifty pounds each, but if you can't drive me, I'm cool."

"Come on, I can't let you lug those things around, it's the least I can do." I grabbed one of the crates and started carrying it to my car. "These are gigantic."

"Oh yeah, these are big mommas," he said, pulling a case beside me. "I sold my dirt bike for these kits. Also, do you think you could drop me off at home afterward? I don't live too far from there."

"…Sure, man," I said, reaching my car and popping the trunk.

During the drive to and from Talent HQ, Chester shared with me what seemed to be his entire life story. In high school, he was a talented dancer and his troupe was invited to perform at the opening ceremony of the Summer Olympics, but weeks before the performance, he got in a car crash that left him in a full body cast. He spent nearly a year of his life in bed, but he received two hundred grand in insurance money, which he used to travel the world and live like a prince until the money dried up eight months later. Chester's ticket into porn came when he answered a Backpage ad offering a chance to "Fuck a Porn Star on the Infamous *Bangbus*." He showed up, got wood, got laid, and got paid. The producers then called him back for another one, and then another after that.

"I made a hundred bucks that first day," he said. "I was like, shit, if I can get paid a hundred bucks just to fuck, I'll do this everyday of my life. Now, I get paid a hundred just to set up lights and move furniture, and when I do perform my fee is a *hard* three-hundred, bro; I'm covered. But I do it for fun; I fucking love porn." His passion reminded me of someone I knew.

Chester lived in a forgotten about part of the valley known as *Winnetka*. I parked out front of his house and helped him unload the lights.

"You wanna come in and hang out for a minute?" he asked. "I just got the new *Call of Duty* and a big ass TV, man, like sixty inches." I hesitated. "I also got some fat blunts rolled," he said.

"…Well, okay," I said, "but I can't stay long."

"Sweet!" he said. "Come on in, man."

Instinctively, I started carrying a case toward the house's separate 1-car garage.

"Oh, no, not in there," Chester said, "a Mexican family lives in there. Yeah, our landlord really stretched every dollar he could with this place."

"…Interesting," I said, shrugging my shoulders and

changing course.

I followed Chester inside. Right away my nostrils were stung by the acrid tang of ammonia.

"Got a cat?" I asked.

"There's a little critter running around here somewhere," he said, and then referring to the case, he added, "Just drop that anywhere."

I looked for a suitable spot. There were pet crates, dirty clothes, and puffed trash bags everywhere. Two sagged and torn leather loveseats faced the room's centerpiece, the aforementioned sixty-inch flat screen TV, all of the surrounding windows covered to enhance the viewing experience.

"Damn, you weren't kidding," I said, stacking the crate against one of the couch's armrests.

"That's my baby, right there," he said with satisfaction.

"So do you live here alone?" I asked.

"Oh no, I have two roommates," he said. "Hey! Have you met *Gavin Long* yet?"

"No, but I think I've heard of him," I said, unaffected, although I was more than aware of Gavin—he's a male performer too. In fact, he was one of the guys I originally reached out to on Twitter. Naturally, he ignored me, but that's neither here nor there.

"Let me curate this," said Chester. "Get you two together; he and his girlfriend *Fiona Fire* both live here; well, right now they're shooting in Vegas, but they'll be back this weekend."

"Cool," I said.

"Go on, make yourself comfortable, I'll be right back," he said, disappearing through the hallway and into his bedroom.

I sat on one of the ripped love seats, being careful not to touch anything. Chester returned with a small and wiry black ferret in his arms; it scampered up his chest and snaked around his neck.

"And this is my other baby," he said. "Say hello to Weezy. Go on," He urged. "You can pet him."

"*Nice Marmot,*" I said, stroking Weezy.

"Actually, this little guy is a ferret," he said with sincerity.

"Oh, I was just quoting a movie."

"…Oh yeah," he said, slightly confused. Then he pulled out a blunt he had tucked behind his ear and said, "About to take this bad boy to the face, what do you say?"

"…Tempting, but—"

"Aw, come on," he said. "Work's cancelled, what else you gotta do today?"

Go home and jack off, I thought.

"All right, you convinced me," I said.

The burning blunt masked the piss, and as Weezy scurried around the couch and burrowed into the leather, Chester described to me his Valentines Day, last year in Las Vegas. In the morning, he fucked his (now ex) girlfriend in their hotel room bed. Then he went to set and partook in a bukkake. Minutes after popping he got a call for an emergency *stunt cock*, so he went to another set and got a handjob. Finally, he went back to his hotel and fucked his girlfriend again, this time on webcam.

"Jesus," I said, "that's like some marathon shit."

"We all have that one thing," he said, without a hint of irony. "At first I thought I was supposed to be a dancer, but then I screwed that up. Then I thought I was going to live off my insurance check forever, but I spent all of that money. Now I finally figured it out. This is my calling." He took a last lingering hit of the roach and stumped out the cherry. "What do you say, you wanna spark up another one?"

"I should probably head back," I said, getting to my feet. "I have some errands to run, laundry and all that."

"All good, man, all good, no worries," he said. Chester took my number and I told him to text me whenever. As I walked to the door, he picked up Weezy and shook his paw goodbye. Imitating the ferret he said, "Don't be a stranger now."

03

A week later, Chester invited me over for dinner and that's when I met Gavin Long and Fiona Fire.

Gavin was tall and bronze, his head a thick mop of curly blonde hair, and his eyes a piercing blue, but there was something unsettling about them, sunken and blood-shot. He looked like an Abercrombie model who lost his way.

Fiona was a free-spirited and polyamorous *burner*; her body adorned with black tattoos. She was a solid head and shoulders above me, her cut stems accounting for 70% of her body. A Jackrabbit *Spirithood* sat atop her partially shaved head, strands of rainbow dyed hair peeking out from underneath.

For dinner, we shared a bottle of Pinot and ate vegan enchiladas prepared by Fiona. At the table, the three roommates reminisced about the otherworldly experiences they'd had on psychedelics.

"I'm a shrooms man, myself," said Chester.

"Fuck that," I said, sharing my nightmare of a trip. "The first and *last*, let me assure you."

"Nah, man, you did it all wrong," Chester said, "no wonder you were so fucked up. Hey, I have a great idea," he said, impassioned. "Come into the woods with me one weekend, and let me be your Sherpa."

"My Sherpa?" I said.

"Uh oh, he's at it again," said Fiona.

"Pay no attention to his advances, Logan," said Gavin. "Chester is *always* trying to get the new boys to do drugs with him in the middle of nowhere. It's all so innocent until he offers one of his 'world famous' back massages, and then before you know it, you got an ass in your cock—"

"*Hey...*" Chester said, familiar with the ruse. "My massages are world famous." Chester turned his attention back to me. "I promise you'll ride the chill-wave."

"I'll keep it in mind," I said.

"If we're on the topic of psychedelics," said Gavin, "and I'm admittedly not a big psychedelic guy, but for my money, Acid is the pinnacle."

"Never done it," I said.

"...We had a feeling," he said, smiling mischievously.

Fiona excused herself and walked into the kitchen, opening the refrigerator. She returned with a small *Hello-Kitty* lunch box, setting the cold tin on the tabletop. She opened it and retrieved a folded piece of aluminum foil, peeling back the edges to reveal tiny squares of paper with pictures of *Oompa Loompas* printed on them. It looked like a small pack of—

"Stamps?" I asked.

"Sunshine," she corrected.

Gavin slid his chair and put his arm around me. "It will change your life," he said.

Fiona stroked my thigh. "Play with us."

I didn't have any excuses; I was freshly single and uninhibited, so why shouldn't I have a little fun with my new friends? If they can do it, so can I.

"Fuck it."

Chester jumped out of his chair. "I'm gonna get my camera!" He said, running toward his bedroom.

The four of us were sitting in the living room when the drug took effect. My body was glowing, energy radiating from every pore; I felt eight feet tall and growing taller with every passing minute of the come-up. I was invincible, ready to take on the world. And I was smiling so hard I thought my cheeks were going to tear.

Gavin and Fiona started making out. Chester hopped off the couch, and with his camera in hand he assumed a shooter's position, knees bent and elbows locked in his gut. He snapped photos as Fiona stroked Gavin.

I watched the action with growing anticipation. Fiona looked at me and then whispered to Gavin. He nodded his head in approval. She crawled over and started rubbing my thighs, kissing me while Gavin ate her out from behind. Fiona unbuckled my pants as Gavin slipped himself inside of her. Chester snapped shots of the spit-roast. Then Fiona turned around and pounced on top of Gavin, riding him in cowgirl. I stripped naked and stroked myself as I watched.

Fiona looked back at me and said, "I want to feel both of you."

She pulled me toward them and told me to stick it inside of her alongside Gavin.

"At the same time?" I asked.

"Do it," she commanded.

I obeyed, pressing my skin against Gavin's and skimming across his shaft as Fiona absorbed me. Almost impossibly, the pieces fit together, and the three of us shared the same body. For a moment, we were one.

Then reality hit. Gavin started losing wood, and frustrated, he wormed out from underneath, pushing us away as he stomped toward the bathroom. The threesome disbanded almost as quickly as it began.

"Did I do something wrong?" I asked.

"No, you're fine," said Fiona. "Ugh, I should go talk to him." She walked away, leaving Chester and I in the living room.

As I sat dumbfounded, I could hear their voices echoing in the bathroom. Suddenly the door flung open and the two of them charged out and into their bedroom, slamming the door closed behind them. Judging by their intensity, I figured we were done having sex for the night. Begrudgingly, I put my pants back on.

"Don't worry about them," Chester said, turning off his camera and replacing the lens cap. "They're occupying different frequencies."

"What the hell does that mean?" I asked.

"It means they fight all the time."

"Oh."

The two of us sat there in silence.

Chester turned to me and studied my face. "You are a wonderful subject," he said. "Really great bone structure."

"…Uh, Thanks," I said.

"Would you mind if I painted you?" he asked.

"Painted me? What, like one of your French girls?"

Chester laughed. "Oh, ha-ha, I got that," he said. "Good one."

"Sure, you can paint me," I said, "but you don't need me to get naked or anything do you?"

"You are perfect as you are."

"Cool," I said, giving a thumbs-up.

Chester opened another bottle of red, and poured us both a glass. He put on an album from the band, *Polica*, and laid a blue tarp across the living room floor. He grabbed a large sketchpad and an old fishermen's tackle box filled with his art supplies—various paintbrushes, pencils, industrial erasers, charcoal, etc. He knelt on the tarp, and placed the pad in his lap, resting his hand on the page and his gaze on me as I relaxed on the couch.

With my body light and my mind at ease, I closed my eyes and let the power of the drug and the vibrations of the music carry me away for the remainder of my trip.

04

I was on my way to set the day I received a phone call—*the* phone call.

On the other line was my mother. She spoke with practiced patience, as if not to upset her blood pressure.

She said, "We know what you do."

Shit.

This day was inevitable; I should have known better; no matter how far you run, the lie always catches up with you. But now, faced with confrontation, I came clean.

Naturally, my parents were a bit disappointed to learn that their baby boy was now an emerging stud, but they were civil about it. They weren't devastated by any means, and they certainly didn't threaten to disown me, or anything like that.

All throughout my life my parents were supportive of my individuality; I was lucky in that way. They never pushed me to play any sports or join any club because there was a legacy to uphold or unfulfilled goals to pursue. They didn't have an agenda for me; they wanted me to feel things out for myself. When I was fourteen and wanted to play drums they bought me my first drum kit, first letting me play in my bedroom, but then swiftly sending me to the garage after one jam session. When I was sixteen and wanted to be an actor they encouraged me to join the drama group, which was where I spent the entirety of my high school career. When I was eighteen and wanted to be a filmmaker, they gave my friends and I full reign of the house, letting us shoot action sequences in the basement and gory death scenes in the bathroom.

At the very least, I would like to think they understood that my decision to "Show (my) penis on the Internet," as my mom said, was not made out of malice or any bottled up resentment.

But one question still lingered: how did they find out?

"Oh, you'll never believe this," she said. "Allie's parents told us."

Apparently, they had printed out various photos of *Logan* and packed them in a manila folder, creating a half-assed dossier. Then they drove to my parent's house, barged in, and threw the folder on the dining room table, sending naked pictures flying everywhere. I guess they felt entitled to oust me as some sort of retribution for breaking their daughter's heart. *The vile porn star must pay.*

My mom took the "evidence" with a grain of salt. Then she called the source to get the truth.

"Just don't lie to us anymore," she said. "Please, that's all we ask." I promised her I wouldn't.

My entering porn, while scandalous, didn't affect

their love for me. So long as I remained safe and healthy, they would be accepting (tolerant) of my new profession. I think they're proud of me so long as I'm proud of myself.

But then I got to thinking: was I proud of myself?

Well, I did chase a dream to California and was renting my own apartment in Los Angeles—Okay, maybe not LA proper, but the Valley still counts. I was making good money, and on top of that; I was now having enough sex to satisfy a Saudi prince.

But I did leave damage in my wake. I packed up and ditched my family, I ghosted on my internship, and I currently had no plans of going back home anytime soon, let alone in time to start my senior year of College. And in other news, my girlfriend dumped me, her parents hated me, and now, for the rest of my life, I would forever be known as the boy who ran away to be a whore.

But now was not the time to dwell on such things. I pulled up out front of the shoot house and composed myself. It was time to go to work.

05

You could give me a million years and I still wouldn't be able to remember my co-star's name, but I'll never forget her appearance. She was tall, lean, and with a heaving bust. Her platinum blonde hair slicked back, and her eyes polished silver.

"Wow, you are something else," I said, extending my hand. "Hi, I'm Logan."

"*You're* my talent?" she sneered, reluctantly offering a cold and lifeless hand as she sized me up, none too impressed with her new boyfriend for the day.

"*Hmph,*" she said, strutting away.

I took the hint and kept to myself until it was my turn at bat, hoping to just make the best of it and get through the scene as quickly as possible.

But as we prepared to shoot stills, she set some ground rules: "Don't kiss me," she said, "and don't touch my hair. Don't expect me to get you hard, and don't try to fuck me if the camera isn't on, K? Oh, and I'm on my period," she continued. "So don't fuck me too hard."

"Why not?" I asked, still processing all of these newfound blockades.

"Because I have a *sponge* in, duh. And I have more shoots this week, so be careful."

I looked at the director as if to say, *what the hell?* He just shrugged his shoulders, suggesting, *what's the big deal? Just fuck her, kid.*

The big deal was that my supposed partner was a true to form ice-queen; she was on the clock, not here for the sex, only the paycheck.

Her disdain left me hopeless. Forget getting a hard-on; she was incongruous with everything that made me vascular, with everything that transformed me into the throbbing *He-Man* I was paid to portray. I was left hyperventilating under the hot lights, the day resting solely on my shoulders.

Everyone's attitude changed the moment wood troubles began. One minute the crewmembers are all my friends, and the next they're shaking their heads in collective aggravation. The director tried to remain calm and sympathetic, but I could read between the lines; the look of frustration on his face was undeniable.

Dripping sweat, I excused myself to the bathroom. "Just give me a minute!" I called out from the toilet seat, trying desperately to squeeze life into my dick. I could hear them out there, talking about me, laughing at me. I couldn't concentrate. All was lost; Logan Pierce was dead in the water. Limp and unable to do my job, I failed. I was sent home with my tail between my legs.

Never in my life did I imagine a day would come where the communication between my mind and my manhood would be severed, especially not after giving up everything and leaving my old life behind to become a bona fide, mother fucking, PORN STAR.

Feeling less than zero, I called Max and told him the bad news. He laughed at me over the phone. "Take it easy," he said. "This was bound to happen sooner or later, kid. Everyone has bad days."

"Not everyone. Not me," I said, sounding like a first-rate amateur.

"*Yes,*" he said. "Even you. Look, they can't all be home runs. But remember, you're only as good as your last scene, understand? You start making this a habit and soon nobody is gonna book you."

"What am I supposed to do?"

"You want a guarantee?" he said. "Go pay a visit to *Dr. Ross.* He'll give you exactly what you need."

Now that I knew failure was a reality, I couldn't afford to lose my edge. So I did what any self-respecting performer would do, and I took out an insurance policy on my career.

06

Dr. Ross ran a shady urgent care clinic in the armpit of the valley. Upon my arrival, one of the "nurses" led me to a neglected examination room. With stale lights and stained walls it resembled something straight out of *Requiem for a Dream*. The nurse took my vitals and then left me alone, sitting anxiously atop the wax paper.

Five minutes later, the doctor walked in, chattering and pre-occupied. "So, Sporto," he said. "I hear you're in dirty movies and you want some medicine, yeah? Well, we can get you fixed up with whatever you need: Viagra, Levitra, Cialis, even *Caverject* if you don't mind jabbing your junk with a needle."

"What? No, that's okay, Doc," I said. "I'll just stick with the pills—the Viagra."

"No problem, Sporto. Whatever you want," he said. "You need anything else? Xanax? Codeine? Maybe some antibiotics; Do you have a scratchy throat? Could be gonorrhea, you know. A shot in the butt and a Z-pack would clear that right up for you."

"No thanks, Doc. I'm fine," I said. "Just the Viagra."

"Sure, sure. Got a script written up right here for you." He handed me the slip of paper. "Just take this to any pharmacy and you'll be good to go. "

Then the doctor opened the door and shooed me out.

"Okay, have fun," he said. "Take care of yourself, Sporto. See you soon."

"Fucking hope not," I said to myself, walking to my car.

I drove to the nearest CVS, and with my new script in hand I approached the pharmacy counter, doing my best to remain calm and inconspicuous in front of the female pharmacist.

"Hi, I just wanted to drop this off," I said.

"Sure, what's the medication?"

Under my breath I muttered, "Uh…Viagra."

"I'm sorry?" she asked.

"**Viagra**," I said, handing her the script.

"Right," she said, confirming my request. "How many pills would you like?"

"Well, how many can I get?"

"The max is ten," She said.

"Okay. That sounds good."

"Just so you're aware, the price will be $220."

"*Shit.* For ten pills?"

"Yes sir."

What choice did I have? Much like the mandatory

14-day STD tests, these pills were necessary if I wanted to succeed: membership fees in order to join the club and live the dream. A small price to pay, I thought.

"Okay," I said. "I'll take it."

Thirty minutes later my prescription was filled and I left with my very first bottle of magic blue pills—my soon to be new best friends and most trusted allies in my male performer utility belt.

Hereafter, all of my on-camera erections would grade nothing short of pharmaceutical.

07

Back to work. I arrived on set while my co-star, *Dixie Diamond*, was taking *pretty girl* stills, posing seductively in lingerie. I went into the bathroom, brushed my teeth, and popped half of a 100-miligram tablet of Viagra.

I played a culinary student hired by Dixie's husband to teach her how to cook in an effort to bring them closer together and rejuvenate their otherwise fizzling marriage. Things began innocently enough; I sliced tomatoes as Dixie heated olive oil in a pan. She listened and watched intently as I explained how cooking can serve as a natural aphrodisiac amongst couples.

Then she came close and whispered in my ear, "How about we just order take-out and I take your pants off instead?"

Gee, let me think.

"Well, when you put it like that," I said. "Sure!"

Dixie dropped to her knees and went to work, everything going according to plan.

The pill served its purpose and kept me hard—almost a little too hard, actually. My pulse spiked, my eyes tightened, and my face flushed as thick cylinders of blue spiraled around my shaft, throbbing from under the skin. So much blood I could feel my heartbeat in my cock.

But, my god, it looked heroic; a sword carved from Valyrian steel, with razor sharp edges designed with one sole purpose: to pierce the flesh.

08

Chester, Gavin, Fiona, and I dropped acid again and took a trip to Hollywood.

With no destination in mind, we wandered the Boulevard, letting the walk of fame come to life in front of our eyes. The stars transformed into a 3-D hologram scroll of credits to a film with the greatest cast-list of all time, and we were the stars, front and center.

Fiona soon got thirsty and started complaining, which annoyed Gavin, so we ducked into *Greco's Pizza* to get her a soda. Inside, three young women of LA sat at a nearby table leaning against the frames of the shop's open windows, sopping their greasy slices with napkins, varying shades of red staining their soda straws.

Suddenly, an arm reached through the window and grabbed one of the girls by the hair, pulling her back and slamming her against the metal and glass.

"Puta bitch!" A voice yelled before disappearing into the night.

"What the fuck?" I said, frozen in fear.

Before I had even the slightest inclination to act, Gavin had darted out of the doors, the drugs transforming him into a goddamn vigilante of justice. He sprinted down Cahuenga and pounced the guy, driving him face first into the concrete. Mounting the woman-beating prick, Gavin unleashed a barrage of elbow strikes to his face, nearly crushing his eye socket. Then a bouncer from a nearby club ran over to break up the fight, pepper-spraying them both in the process. The men rolled away, writhing in pain, police sirens blaring in the distance.

Gavin staggered to his feet, and in between sobs he screamed, "Water! Water!"

He burst back into the pizza shop. "My eyes!" he yelled. "I'm fucking blind!"

The employees took pity on him, leading Gavin behind the counter toward an already filled sink where he quickly dunked his head, bubbles rushing to the surface as he stomped his feet on the cracked tile floor.

All three women clapped and cheered, celebrating their man. Fiona rolled her eyes and sipped her soda.

"Holy shit," I said, putting my arm around Chester's shoulder. "Guy's a hero."

And with pupils as big as saucers he turned to me and said, "You better believe it. You're with the cool kids now."

09

Max called. "Hey, Pierce," he said, "wanna do a *gangbang?*"

I hesitated. A gangbang? That's some serious shit; it's a contact sport in this business. "Um, I don't know, Max," I said. "'I've never done anything like that before."

"You could use the experience," he said. "I'm gonna book it. It'll be easy. Trust me. They'll pay you a full rate."

"How much is a full rate?" I asked.

"Six-hundred for the day," he said. "It'll be a breeze."

"…Okay, cool," I said, and as simple as that, I agreed to perform in my first professional gangbang. I thought the experience would be awakening, and that it would elevate me to the next tier of the male performer hierarchy. After this I'd be considered one of the guys; Allie would be so proud.

Max sent the call-sheet. Outside of myself, the gangbang would consist of five other male performers: *Chris Toker, Michael Anthony, Elvis Bone, Daniel Tame,* and *Marco Del Toro*; all heavy hitters, each with years of experience.

In his youth, Elvis Bone resembled Fabio, with his long golden locks of hair and his well-exercised physique, but now, in his later years, he's weathered and his body undisciplined, gravity getting stronger with each passing day. Chris Toker has a dick that's almost unforgettable; it's extremely long but awkwardly pencil-thin. Marco Del Toro is a ripped Latino with a perpetual shit-eating grin and a lower abdomen tattoo of the name "Bella" bordered by a heart. Michael Anthony didn't speak a word of English, and he always wore sunglasses and construction boots in every one of his scenes. Daniel Tame, now twenty-six, had been in the business since he was eighteen. He practically grew up in porn. Much later, I would learn that Daniel was no stranger to the drug Caverject—an intravenous dick stimulant. One day he would inject just a little too much juice into his shaft, causing his dick to inflate like a balloon. He'd have to be rushed to the hospital to have it drained before it ruptured. The events of that day would force him into early retirement, but I digress.

All six of us were being brought together to feast upon the voracious Nina Knives. Since our last encounter, Nina had become renowned for the elasticity of her asshole; at least that's what I saw on Twitter. I had recently seen a clip of Nina inserting the barrel of a *Louisville Slugger* inside herself. God only knows where you go from there; I guess a six-man gangbang was only appropriate.

On the day of, I reported to set, which a dilapidated warehouse deep in the valley. I introduced myself to the guys, and gave Nina a familiar hug. At that point it was made abundantly clear to me that I was the smallest person in the cast; all of the guys were each at least six-feet tall and nearly two hundred pounds, while I stood at five-foot-six and was a wet one-hundred and forty. I was even shorter than Nina who stood at five-foot-ten in her high-heels. Already I felt a small sense of inferiority but I tried not to let it bother me. I filled out my paperwork, popped my pill, and soon it was time.

The set was a cheap classroom; six school desks placed haphazardly in front of a barren teacher's desk with a double-sided chalk board behind it bearing the word: "**DETENTION**."

On action, the guys and I were sitting at the desks. We were a surly bunch, all serving time for various infractions. Nina entered carrying a yardstick. She strutted around the room, trying to intimidate us with hard glares and empty threats, but they only served to feed our rowdiness. Frustrated, Nina stood in front of the class and whacked her desk with the yardstick, nearly breaking it in two. The sound cut through our chatter and reverberated in the silence. With a firm tone, Nina asserted we were all in *deep* trouble and in need of some serious discipline. We sneered, but Nina stood her ground.

"Fine," she said, changing tact and unbuttoning her blazer. "Is this what it takes to get through to you knuckle-heads?" She ripped open her blouse, exposing her scholarly tits. Everyone was slack-jawed; she now had our attention. "That's better," she said. "Now, are you boys ready to follow instruction?"

We nodded our heads in agreement, unable to break our stare.

"Good boys," she said. "Now, everyone, take out your cocks. I'm going to come by and examine each one at your desk."

We did as we're told. Nina walked around the room, blowing us one by one.

That was the fun part.

The director yelled, "Cut! Nina, get on the desk. Guys, get naked and circle her."

Everyone disrobed. I had some slight trouble untying my knotted shoelaces, and my pants got stuck around my ankles, which successfully took me out of the fantasy. My wood started to recede and I was getting softer by the second. Typically, I find kissing to be one of the most effective ways to keep my edge; I like the intimacy of it. In this case, however, I realized that making out with Nina while she was busy with five other dicks was definitely out of the question, especially after I glanced over and saw her giving Elvis a rim-job.

Fuck no.

But, being a young mastermind, I had a great idea; I'd pop another pill. I figured if I doubled up, I'd be twice as hard. Fucking genius. I ran off set to my duffel bag and rummaged through to find my prescription bottle.

Behind me I heard the director yell, "Action!" and the guys went to work. I looked at the group and made eye contact with the director whose flailing arm and pointed finger were a strong indication for me to *get the fuck in there.*

Now, there is a grace period with dick pills; a user has to wait at least fifteen minutes for the drug to enter the bloodstream and take effect, but as legend has it, you can expedite the process by holding the pill under your tongue until it dissolves. Panicked, I decided to fast track my results, so I tossed the entire pill into my mouth and crushed it between my teeth like it were a *SweeTart.* Unsurprisingly, the taste of Viagra is the farthest thing from candy. My face puckered, and I gagged, fighting every urge I had to spit it out, but it quickly turned into a chalky paste and I had no choice but to swallow it, tonguing the remaining muck out of my molars.

Threading needle, I approached the desk but didn't quite know where to stand; everyone had their legs spread wide, so in order for me to squeeze in I had to step over or in between pairs of hairy legs, and rub shoulders with the other guys as we all jacked off in unison. Nina did her best to service us all; when she wasn't getting fucked, she was sucking one or two or three cocks, which caused her to drool onto the desk. That pooling spit then dripped onto the floor, squishing under our heels and between our toes. Then Michael Anthony— wearing his goddamn steel-toe boots—stepped on my foot and nearly crushed my frail bones.

This is where things began to unravel.

My veins started to throb, all right; I could feel them

practically bursting out of my temples. There was a tingle in my arm and leg started twitching. My heart raced, beads of sweat simmering on my forehead.

Two pills were a bad idea.

My vision clouded and the room became a dizzying blur. I thought I was about to faint, so I stepped out of frame, retreating from the circle, and sitting down at one of the discarded desks to catch my breath.

From there, I watched the rest of the action unfold in front of me. The scene was an absolute feeding frenzy. Nina lay on her back and each man took a turn before spinning her around to a fellow classmate. The men spit on her, slapped her, and called her names. Soon they were double penetrating her, and then even *triple penetrating* her—something I never thought possible until now. It was one thing to watch this type of action on my computer alone in my bedroom, but to actually witness it in person, to be a *participant*; it scared me.

Bewildered, I sat there hopelessly jacking off as the seasoned veterans proved their worth, Nina taking everything with a smile. On the surface, she appeared helpless and at the mercy of the pack, but in reality, she remained in control, encouraging the massacre and orchestrating the dance. The master of the meat puppets.

A gangbang is an art form, something I was not yet ready to understand.

The director yelled, "Cut! Nina, get on the floor. Guys, cum on her face."

One by one, each guy approached Nina and dropped his seed. I tightly closed my eyes and focused on better days. Miraculously, I worked up the courage to run toward her and add to the already plastered canvas.

Then I got dressed, grabbed my check, and drove home without saying goodbye to anyone, ready to smoke this day away.

10

I was at the Winnetka house in Chester's bedroom. With stained skin and dirty fingernails, he showed me the first pass of the portrait. It was a dark, moody, and somewhat disturbing rendering of my bare skull. There I was, void of skin and hair, hollow eyed and reduced to white smears on black charcoal.

"Isn't it haunting?" he said. "You have to start with the structure, the bones; you have to get underneath the skin before you can really depict the face. I like the ambiguity of the skull; no gender, race, or creed, just good old fashion natural selection gazing back at you."

The kid definitely had heart, I'll give him that; it was more than I could ever hope to make, I can't draw for shit, let alone do it on psychedelics.

The front door opened and Gavin stormed in, yelling into his cell phone. He and Fiona were having problems again. He paced around the living room and kitchen, and from Chester's bedroom I could make out a few disgruntled sighs, grumbles, and the occasional, "That's fucking bullshit!"

Lowering his voice, Chester confided in me how tired he was of these arguments. "They're just so narrow-minded," he said. "And I always tell them, 'if you're searching for answers, take mushrooms because they are here to lead us and reveal the truth within ourselves. But, you know, most people are afraid of facing their true selves, so…"

"And you're not?" I asked, playing devil's advocate.

"I can't afford to be," he said, prodding his temple. "I got too much shit in here I need to figure out."

From the kitchen, Gavin shouted and I heard the shattering of glass and plastic against the tile floor. He stomped past Chester's room and into his own. "Goddammit!" he screamed, slamming his door, the wood bouncing off the frame and rattling as it settled ajar.

"Think we should talk to him?" I asked.

"You can go if you want," he said.

And a part of me did, so I crept through the hallway and spied through the open door. Gavin was rifling through the top drawer of his dresser. He found a small wooden box and set it on the glass surface of his computer desk.

I knocked. "Hey, man," I said.

"Logan!" he said. "Good to see you, I didn't know you were here."

"Everything cool?" I asked.

"Peachy-fucking-keen," he said. "Come in, come in. Close the door."

I did as he asked and sat on the foot of his bed, which

were actually two mattresses stacked on top of one another. Gavin open the box and dug through its contents.

"You like to ski?" he asked.

"Ski?" I said. "Uh, I did it once with my parents in the Poconos; I guess I'd consider myself more of a snowboarder if anything."

"No, not ski," he said, shaking his head. He looked at me while tapping his nostril. "*Ski*. You know, Candy Mountain, booger sugar."

"…Cocaine?" I asked.

"Fresh powder," he said, brandishing a tiny vial of crystalline white. He uncapped it and poured a small mound onto the glass. With his credit card he methodically cut and re-staked the drug until it was soft and fine. Then he split it up into thick lines. He took a twenty-dollar bill out of his wallet and rolled it into a tight cylinder. He put the bill into his nostril, and with a hearty snort, one of the lines disappeared. He recoiled and held his nose, extending the bill to me. "Wanna hit the slopes?" he asked, sniffling in quick bursts.

It might be hard to believe, but I'd never tried coke before. I guess I'd seen too many movies with characters snorting lines, their eyes going wide and their teeth grinding. Then they always wind up aggressive, unstable, and strung out by the end, so I was never really itching to use it.

And yet, at this moment my curiosity got the better of me. "Sure, why not," I said.

"That'a boy," Gavin said, handing me the bill.

I grabbed it and approached the desk. I stuck the bill into my right nostril, bent down to the powder, and snorted. The granules scraped my nasal passage on the way up, mixing with mucous and coating the back of my throat with a bitter drip. I felt like I had to puke, but I kept swallowing to avoid it.

"Lick your finger," he said, "Collect the dust and rub it into your gums."

I did. My gums tingled and soon my entire mouth went numb.

Gavin patted my shoulder in contentment. "I fucking love gummies," he said.

I could feel the drug coursing through my body. My muscles tightened, my fists clenched, and my synapses were firing. I was electric.

Two lines later, Gavin and I were sitting on his bed trading war stories and commiserating at rapid pace about the difficulties of maintaining a relationship in porn.

"She called me an enabler," he said. "Which is pretty fucking ironic given her love for psychedelics. So, I called her hypocrite, and she fucking hung up on me."

"You gonna call her back?" I asked.

"Whatever," he said, feigning indifference, but I could sense this wasn't the first time he let his emotions get the better of him. "I don't even care, really. I've been here too many times before. You know, I've been in the business three years, and the longest 'relationship' I've had was less than three months; just a few short weeks before it all crashed and burned. They always do, and yet I never seem to learn."

"We are slaves to our *little* heads, aren't we?" I said.

"Fuckin-A," he said, prepping more lines. "But, hey, this is best place to be for guys like us, you know? There's fresh pussy every single day; we're in Porno-land, for Christ's sake! We shouldn't be tied down. We should be fucking as many chicks as possible. *Carpe Diem* and all that shit." He snorted his line and handed me the bill.

"Here, here!" I said, taking the money and the drugs.

Maybe I was just sharp and streamlined, but Gavin's words shined with great brilliance. At my fingertips was a sea of young, nubile, and sexually ripe women just waiting to be *pierced*, most of them a phone call, a text, or a simple tweet away. I'd be a fool not to take advantage.

It was time for me to start having some fucking fun.

11

While innocently scrolling through Twitter with no predisposition whatsoever, I came across the profile of a new burgeoning starlet by the name of *Monroe Blue*. With caramel skin and golden hair, Monroe had a feline presence about her, something resembling an adolescent lioness: spunky and unpredictable. She stood at five-foot even and weighed ninety-five pounds—the quintessential bubble-gum blonde spinner.

After a few calculated *likes* of her posts, Monroe finally noticed me, which led her to peruse my profile, ensnaring herself in my web and ensuring her next step, an immediate follow-back. Through direct messages, it was quickly made apparent that the two of would get along just fine.

She asked, "Do you shoot *content?*"

Content is a quid-pro-quo style of porn in which performers shoot a scene under the agreement that all parties involved take ownership of the footage, so they can edit and distribute it independently and at will. It's a way for performers to own their own material and sell it through clip stores, private buyers, or through their personal website.

Or in my case, it can be used as an excuse for performers to fuck each other.

"Absolutely," I said, offering my phone number. "Hit me up anytime."

Saturday morning, I received the text I had been waiting for. Monroe was on the hunt for a stunt-cock to appear in an amateur P.O.V boy/girl scene for her website. And not just any cock—she wanted *mine*. I was already hard at the thought. With haste, I accepted her offer like the eager lap dog that I am.

"You can come over later once my hangover is gone," she said.

In the meantime, I ate breakfast, worked out, and watched porn to edge myself, working up to orgasm and then staving off at the last second to effectively compound my climax.

3:00 p.m. I texted Monroe. No response.

5:00 p.m. Radio Silence.

6:00 p.m. Maybe she had forgotten about me, I thought. Maybe she went and found someone new. So be it. Onward and upward.

Then I received a text from another female performer, *Becky Bolt*. Becky was sultry with an air of sophistication and class. Her brunette hair was long and wavy, her eyes emerald green. Earlier in the week Becky and I were scene partners. On action, we sat poolside, whispering sweet nothings before ravaging one another in front of the cameras. It was a rather pleasant afternoon in the Valley.

"I've got a bottle of Cabernet and loads of pent up aggression," said Becky. "I need to have the *brat* dominated out of me. Think you can help?"

I quickly realized there was little point in waiting for Monroe; if she wanted me she would've responded by now. There were plenty of other women out there, and right now Becky was soaked to the bone, offering herself on a silver platter; all I'd have to do is take the initiative.

So, letting my little head take the driver seat, I made new plans.

"I could be of service," I said.

"Good," she said. "Pick me up tonight at ten."

I hopped in the shower, and while under the steaming water I heard the distinct tone of a new text message. I dried off, draped myself in a towel, and checked my phone. It was Monroe.

"Hey, sexy man," she said. "All Better now. How's 8 looking? I'm ready for you."

Shit. I was at a crossroads. On the one hand, the girl I had been drooling over wanted to use me as her personal boy-toy, but on the other, I had just planned a play-date with my new friend. My options were binary. Either I choose to spend time with one lucky lady and ditch the loser, or I could attempt one of the greatest dating feats known to man, a challenge reserved for only the highest echelon of bachelors and sexual mavens; *The Double Feature.*

I texted Monroe. "I'm all yours."

The plan was simple. I was going to dick-n-dash Monroe, pick up Becky, bring her back to my apartment, and discipline her in the confines of my bedroom.

8:15 p.m. I arrived at Monroe's apartment in Woodland Hills. We exchanged pleasantries and she took my hand and led me upstairs to her bedroom. She slipped off her yoga-pants, picked up her iPhone and started recording. She told me to eat her pussy while pressing her up against the wall. Assuming the position, I dropped to my knees, devouring her like a starving mutt. Monroe passed me the camera and crawled to the floor, unbuckling my belt and pulling down my jeans. I shot P.O.V. footage as she went to work, with thick lines of spit falling from her mouth, tangling in her hands, and dribbling onto her chest. With her face wet and lips tender, she stood and arched against the wall, inviting me inside. I shot more footage as we fucked prison style, her arms behind her back and my pants around my ankles. She slinked away with the camera, crawling into bed and turning on her side. I followed behind her, curling into her back. She came, and then it was my turn. She received it in spades due to my earlier regime, strings of glossy white across her torso and up to her neck. Monroe blew a kiss to the camera and then cut it. The two of us laid together in silence, our hearts beating in rhythm as we caught our breath. She grabbed a pack of baby wipes, and we took a bird bath. She promised to email me the footage and treat me to dinner one night soon for taking the time out of my busy schedule to come over. Sex first, and then dinner. I like that.

9:30 p.m. I jumped in my car and raced into North Hollywood where Becky was killing time in a local bar down the street from her apartment. She met me out-front, and as I pulled up, my headlights illuminated her diamond-studded high-heels and her black leather romper, cut just short enough to expose the creases of her cheeks.

"Fucking finally," Becky said, opening the passenger door and swiftly taking a seat. I could tell she was in a mood; she must've been drinking whiskey. The brat was in full effect.

Not to worry, though. With a smile, I happily accepted the challenge.

At my apartment, I forewent grabbing wine glasses in favor of just drinking straight from the bottle, Hemingway style. We disappeared into my bedroom. I pushed Becky onto the sheets and straddled her back. I caressed her skin, squeezing her shoulders and working down the muscles along her spine. I could feel her cold demeanour subsiding and her body submitted to my hands. Together, we found the knots troubling her. I told her to take a deep breath and while she exhaled I pressed even harder. She grimaced and I could hear her whimper; yet she still continued to push her back against me, wanting me to dig deeper, longing to be put in her place. Becky liked the pain. In the pain all of her worries and petty troubles disappeared. In the pain she felt alive.

I wrapped my hands around Becky's throat and applied pressure, bending her back toward me and resting her forehead on my lips so I could stare into her eyes. She gasped and I grabbed the lot of her hair and pulled her back further, matching our lips together. We kissed and sucked face and slobbered all over each other like rabid swine. I pulled Becky off the bed and onto the floor, kneeling her in front of my full-length closet mirror. I pulled out my cock and she attacked it with fervor. "Keep your hands at your side," I said, squaring her head and thrusting in and out of her mouth, watching the action unfold in the reflection. Becky remained on her knees and I wormed behind her. We fucked doggy style, Becky using the glass for support. I stuck two fingers in either side of her mouth and fish-hooked her, pulling her cheeks apart to expose her teeth.

Then I got to my feet and stood over Becky. Shining with sweat and makeup running down her face, she played with her pussy and watched in awe as I stroked myself until I covered her image in the mirror. She licked the glass clean, savoring the taste and swallowing every last drop.

With drying specks on her lips, Becky looked up at me and said, "Thank you, sir. Now buy me pizza, please!"

We went into the living room and smoked a joint as we finished the wine. The pizza soon arrived and we ate while cuddling together on the couch. An hour later, Becky Uber'd back to her apartment, and I went straight to bed, content with a job well done.

Without showering, without brushing my teeth, without changing my clothes, and without even a swig of mouthwash, I drove directly from one girl to the next; two shows in one night. This was the fantasy; *this* was the dream.

And to think, I did it all without the help of Viagra. The animal was now loose and on the prowl.

Logan Pierce was back.

12

Remy St. Martin and I met at work. I fucked her in the ass and fell in lust. She confided a fantasy in which she is taken into a back alleyway and mercilessly fucked by a group of savages in black tuxedos and ivory gloves. She was bred for porn; her career superseded everything else, besides getting high, of course. She would wake and bake like a pro, chasing blunt after blunt after blunt. I tried my best, but I couldn't keep up.

Stella Staxx had a boyfriend when we first met, but she said they were in an open relationship. I met up with her one night while she was dog sitting at a friend's house. We smoked. We made out. I stopped in the middle of it and told her I didn't feel right about the whole thing. She said my moral compass was refreshing. Shortly thereafter, I changed my mind and we fucked anyway. Somehow word gets out that we hooked up, and I learn her relationship isn't as open as she claimed. By some freak circumstance we're later booked together in an anal scene. I thought it an effective conclusion.

Sabrina Wolff also had a boyfriend when we first met but that didn't stop us. She had a big scar on her inner thigh.

"Ninja attack," she said at first, before eventually admitting the truth. She used to get off on *cutting*, and while doing a live cam-show a couple years back she accidentally cut herself a little too deep, blood seeping into her carpet and staining the fibers a deep rust before the ambulance finally arrived. Must've been one hell of a show.

Cherry Pain and I met on Twitter. After a brief dialogue, I took her out to dinner. Unbeknownst to me, Cherry was binging on *Oxycontin*, and she fell asleep at the table. Embarrassed, I took her home, and when I walked inside her apartment I met her roommate, fellow performer, *Gina Hazel*. I put cherry to bed and decided to stay for a bit. Later, Gina and I fucked on the living room floor; talk about making a strong first impression. All things considered, it was a pretty good night.

Mandy Madison and I also met on Twitter. Mandy was eighteen-years-old and hailed from a small town in middle-of-nowhere, Virginia. Mandy's face was round, smooth, and peppered with cute little freckles. She stood a couple inches taller than me, and her plump and meaty thighs accounted for the bulk of her weight. Mandy's skin was another story altogether. On the Internet, it appeared soft and creamy, but in person, the illusion of Photoshop quickly gave way. Mandy's shoulders were dry and cracked, almost even craterous. This newfound perspective didn't exactly thrill me, but Mandy was bubbly and poised to be a joy in the sack, so I maintained. At my apartment, we stripped and I kissed my way from her lips to her neck and down to her chubby breasts and lower down toward her groin only to discover, with a flooding sense of nausea, that her little teenage pink pussy had a wretched, rotten, no good, awful stench emanating from within. It was rancid, invasive, and unlike anything I had ever smelled before, but why should that have stopped me, right?

Chelsea Marx and I met at a porn party in Hollywood hosted by Ron Jeremy, who, believe it or not, is actually a lot fatter in person. Gavin and I went together and spent most of the night sneaking away into the bathroom to do key-bumps. When we weren't skiing, we were pounding tequila shots and scouting for *talent*. That's when I spotted Chelsea, drinking like there was no tomorrow. We lured her into the bathroom, and the three of us locked ourselves away. I did three, maybe four bumps, and then Gavin and I both did a line off of Chelsea's tits for good measure. Gavin stuck his tongue in her mouth and I licked her tits clean of any residual powder, rubbing her pussy through her clothes. Chelsea knelt down and started sucking me. Gavin rubbed himself from outside his pants; Chelsea urged him to take them off, but he refused, acting coy. Sweating, he stuck his hand in his pants and fapped harder. Chelsea persisted in convincing him to get naked, but he got annoyed and pushed her away.

"Leave me alone," he said.

"Whoa, take it easy," I said, reaching my arm to his shoulder. "What's wrong—"

"Fuck off," he said, swatting my arm and walking

away. "Nothing's wrong. I just need a fucking drink."

Ruining yet another threesome, Gavin lumbered out of the bathroom, leaving Chelsea and I alone, but I didn't care; I was high and horny in Hollywood.

"Well, looks like it's you and me," I said, turning my attention back to Chelsea who now had her hand over her mouth. "Uh oh," I said. "What's up?"

Chelsea rushed to the toilet, throwing her head into the bowl. Cock hard and pants around my ankles, I toddled over and held her hair, aiming her mouth as she purged her drinks, her dinner, and whatever else may have been occupying her stomach. Then she washed her mouth out and we returned to the party, going our separate ways. We haven't seen or spoken to each other since.

13

I woke up one morning to a rather unusual surprise in the form of a small red bump on my ass. It was the diameter of a dime and tender to the touch—just a pimple, I thought, so I decided to ignore it, hoping it would clear up and go away on it own.

But it remained, and it grew and grew, and grew, filling with brown fluid and bloating like a rotten cherry tomato. It became such a heaping mass that it sunk my right ass-cheek about half an inch lower than my left. It was near impossible to put any weight on my right foot without unbearable pain shooting up my spine. I couldn't walk and I sure as shit couldn't sit down.

I was fucked.

About the time it became a pulsating ulcer, I decided I should probably visit the doctor, and being that I didn't have health insurance or rapport with anybody else in town, I found myself once again crawling to Dr. Ross.

At his office, I was escorted into another neglected room. The doctor came in, and I pulled down my pants to reveal the unwanted houseguest.

"Oh, boy," he said. "That's a big one." And without so much as a lingering observation he determined it was *Staph-infection*.

"Yessir, no doubt about it," he said. "That's a nasty little gusher, isn't it? Not a problem, though. I can lance that right away, Sporto, get you out of here lickety-split."

"Son of a bitch," I said, cursing myself. "How could this happen?"

"Oh this is pretty common," he said. "You know, you get these girls coming from bumblefuck nowhere to shoot porn, and they're doing all kinds of drugs and then they get infections, their skin breaks, their teeth rot, and then they're out there sucking and fucking everything. Everyone's sharing each other's juices, it's like a little kid's playground."

"That's very reassuring, Doc," I said.

"Yeah, well that's why you have me, Sporto," he said, patting me on the back. "Okay, take your pants off and lie on your stomach."

I followed orders and the doctor sterilized the boil with rubbing alcohol, surrounding it with a perimeter of gauze. He unsheathed a small scalpel. "Try and breathe through the pain," he said, right before slicing the gusher in half, spewing blood and puss.

And in a blink, all the pain disappeared. I felt euphoric as he gripped the bloody flesh with his gloves and drained every last drop of infectious fluid. It's the same revolting pleasure one gets from popping a massive zit, squirts of yellow cream shooting onto the bathroom mirror, and loving every second of it with a twisted smile.

14

Nikki Sinn and I were co-stars. The scene was sloppy, rabid, and aggressive. It wasn't supposed to be an anal scene, but Nikki demanded I stick it in her ass.

The director shrugged. "Look, I ain't gonna pay you extra for it," he said. "But if you wanna do it, by all means."

Nikki swung her legs over her head, saying, "rail me, *fuck-boy!*"

What's a boy to do?

After the romp, Nikki and I exchanged numbers. A couple days later while I was out running errands, she gave me a call. "Hey Fucker," she said. "What are you doing?"

"I'm in the car," I said.

"You should let me suck your cock."

"Oh really?"

"I'm at a shoot house in the Hills," she said. "Come pick me up, fuck-boy."

"I'll be there in fifteen," I said, realizing I am indeed a slave to my urges.

I drove to a house on Wonderland Avenue. Nikki was standing on the curb dressed in platform heels, a red miniskirt, and a wrinkled white button down knotted in the front. Her bleached blonde hair was done up in haphazard pigtails, and her garish knock-off sunglasses masked her face. Slung across her shoulders was a stuffed yellow duck backpack.

"Hi, Mr. Peerzzz," she slurred, falling into my passenger seat, her cheap perfume filling the car. She reached over and gave the crotch of my jeans a hearty squeeze. Leaning closer, she stuck her tongue in my mouth, alcohol reeking on her breath.

"Have a Good Scene?" I asked.

"Fucked za *shit* out of a lady-boy," she said, "My ass got pummeled by tranny dick!"

Nikki opened her backpack, unzipping the ducks stomach to reveal a plastic fifth of *Tito's*. She unscrewed the cap and turned up the bottle, letting the sterile liquid spill over her cheek. She wiped her face, opened her window, and hocked a loogie toward a parked Porsche.

"Goddamn," I said. "You're on one today, huh?"

"Just drive, Fuck-boy," she said.

I probably should've been more cautious, but Nikki's attitude turned me on; she was foul and obscene, the perfect candidate to appease my depravity. I began growing at the thought and Nikki took notice. She unbuckled my pants and pulled me out, sucking as I sped around the winding canyon roads.

At home, we didn't even make it to the bed, she attacked me in the kitchen, dropping to her knees and tearing off my jeans. I fucked her mouth as spit fell onto the linoleum. She pulled me to the floor, lifted her skirt, and sat on my face, forcing me to worship her dirty asshole. She slid down my chest and slipped my cock inside of her with ease, riding me in reverse cowgirl until my tailbone was bruised.

Nikki grabbed her duck and unzipped its belly. She pulled out a floppy double-sided pink dildo. She sucked on one end as other flailed against her tits. Slapping my thigh, she said, "Spread your legs."

"What!?" I shrieked.

"Come on, don't be a little bitch-boy," she said. "Now that you've had *my* ass, you must give me yours."

Holy. Shit. What had I gotten myself into? Before I could even process the situation, Nikki hopped off and pulled my legs up over my head.

"Hey, listen," I said. "I've never done—"

"Shut up and stroke your cock," she said.

I had never once been on the receiving end, but I'd be lying if I said a part of me wasn't at least a little bit curious. I wondered if that was an effect of having too much sex. Was I beginning to lose interest in the things that once brought me pleasure? Was I so eager to entertain this because it broke the monotony? Would I now have to keep upping the ante to keep myself satisfied?

No matter, I played along and jacked off as Nikki dug her face between my cheeks, priming me for what was about to come: the first insertion, her index finger. My eyes shot open and I breathed through my teeth. It was peculiar, undoubtedly a new sensation, but one finger wasn't so bad. Then she added a second. I clenched and Nikki spanked me.

"Open up!" she demanded.

"Sorry," I said.

"This is my hole now," she said. "And I want it nice and loose for me."

I kept stroking but fought to concentrate as Nikki continued licking and spitting and fingering until she felt I was open enough.

"You're now ready for my friend," she said, as a matter of fact.

"Uh…are you sure?" I asked.

Nikki spanked me again, harder this time. "Don't talk," she said. "Be a good little fuck-boy and let my friend join."

Nikki grabbed the toy and spit on it. I nervously panted as she brought it closer and pressed it against my hole, pushing until my skin parted. I gasped as she thrust and split me open. Wincing, I begged Nikki to go slow, but my pleas went ignored. She prodded deeper, making me squirm in pain with every inch, taking pride in punishing the pervert. Eventually my ass clinched too tight for her to continue, and the second she removed the toy I put my legs back on the ground, withdrawing.

"Please, no more," I said. "It fucking hurts."

"You're a little bitch," Nikki said, fuming. "Fine.

What would *you* like to do?"

Right now my asshole was on fire and I wanted nothing more than to nurse myself on a block of ice.

"Um, well, I guess I'd still like to cum," I said.

"Do you now?" she said with searing apathy. "I *would've* let you cum inside my pussy; my uterus is fucked anyway, but that's something reserved for men. Since you don't want to play by my rules, you can jerk yourself onto your stomach like the bitch-boy you are."

Emasculated, I decided against it.

As I got dressed, Nikki dug back into the duck and found a half-drunk bottle of water; at least it looked like water. She opened it and poured a capful of the clear liquid. She shot it back, and her head sprang as her face puckered.

"What the hell is that?" I asked.

"Fucking GHB," she said, sucking through her teeth. "I'm ready to fucking party."

Jesus.

"I need a ride into Sylmar," she said. "You gonna drive me?"

It was 4:45 pm on a Tuesday afternoon, a future of standstill traffic with Nikki wailing in my ear projected in my mind. I considered it for a millisecond before saying, "That's not happening."

"Fucking cunt," she said. "Don't expect to fuck me ever again."

"How about I split an Uber with you?"

"Prince Fucking Charming," she said, oozing you know what.

I didn't care; I would've paid for a black-car just to get rid of her. Soon her ride came and Nikki was out the door. Then I sulked into my bedroom, jacked off in front of my computer, and washed the motherfucking egg off my face.

15

I went to Talent HQ to get tested. I paid the obligatory $165 testing fee, peed in a cup, and gave my blood. The next morning I expected an email with a link containing the PDF of my negative results, but it never came. Instead, I got a phone call—another *fucking* phone call.

Turns out, I tested positive for gonorrhea.

I didn't want to believe it. I didn't feel any different, and I certainly didn't feel *sick*. But change was coming. It all began with a drip, sticky and green. It oozed like snot and made me feel like I had to pee every ten seconds, but I didn't, I couldn't because of the pain; a ball of spines nestled in my urethra like an urchin stuck inside a sea cucumber. And still, I continued to drip and drip.

Dr. Ross welcomed me back with open arms and dollar signs in his eyes. He knew why I was there; he had been expecting this.

In the examining room, I dropped my pants and shifted my weight to one leg. Behind me, the doctor prepped a shot, the sinister flick of a *very* large syringe being unmistakable. I could've sworn I saw him smirk right before he jabbed me, shooting a barrage of nuking antibiotics straight into my ass and then firmly rubbing my cheek with a gloved hand to secure even distribution. He slapped on a Band-Aid, and I pulled up my pants, following him to the front desk. He gave me a cocktail of pills to take home—a "Z-pak," as he called it. $130 later, I was on my way.

Work was cancelled, money was lost, and for the next eight days I was relegated to the *injured* list where I endured daily discharge, explosive diarrhea, and a spreading sense of disillusion.

Ignoring my extra-curricular activities, I can't even begin to imagine how much blood, sweat, spit, vomit, piss, shit, and cum is stained into the carpets and couches on set. Some of the shoot-houses have been around since the nineties, with two decades worth of jizz seeped in to love seat cushions.

The truth is, this industry is laden with filth. STD's are a constant, looming dark cloud. Sooner or later we all get sick. It's not a question of *if*, but of when and how severe.

And I know, the imminent catching of disease should've been a clear sign of danger; a good enough reason for me to walk away and call it quits, but I didn't. I took it in stride. Like the dick pills and like the staph infection, I resolved that STD's were nothing more than extra baggage; just a reality of life in the business.

16

I decided to take it easy on the careless hook ups. Sure, the life of a bachelor was stimulating and casual sex is great and all, but at the end of the day it's meaningless, just another warm body with which I use to masturbate. It gave me something to do but never quite got me anywhere except the doctor's office. I was tired of the game. I wanted something longer lasting, something devoted, and something pure.

That's when I met *Staci Fox*. Staci was the sweetest teenybopper southern belle I had ever seen, and she was as hungry as they come. Her Georgian drawl was soft, angelic, and her crystal blues screamed innocence and naivety. We spent the whole day cuddling, whispering, teasing, wrestling, massaging, petting, and kissing long before the cameras ever started rolling. Puppy love.

After we got our checks, I drove Staci to the model house she was staying at. I carried in her bags and she led me to her bedroom. Closing the door, she slipped out of her pants and tossed away her shirt. I pressed her up against the wall, my hand resting on her throat as she wrapped her legs around my waist.

The LA County Fair was in town. I planned to go with the *Cool Kids* and drop acid. I thought it would be a perfect first date for Staci and I. After getting dressed, I drove us to meet up with Chester and the couple—who had patched things up for the time being. I introduced Staci, and they all fawned over her, it was hard not to.

In the parking lot, each one of us dropped a tab of acid before unleashing ourselves onto the unsuspecting fairgoers and carnies, surrendering to the vivid lights and zippering rides, each moment so full of life and immeasurable possibility.

Chester rode the Gravitron five consecutive times. Gavin won Fiona a giant stuffed penguin and she thanked him with a blowjob in the back seat of the car.

Meanwhile, Staci and I rode the Ferris wheel. Secluded in our suspended car, I reached down toward her warmth and peeled her lips apart, slipping in two fingers, my forehead pressing against hers, her doe-eyes seeking affirmation. "That's a good little fox," I said, gripping the back of her neck and kissing her, the two of us melting together.

The rising sun woke us as it gleamed through my bedroom window. We rolled around, showering each other with kisses. I nibbled her shoulder and her body relaxed, aligning perfectly with mine. She offered her neck and I sunk my teeth, sending shivers down her spine and goose bumps along her skin. I cupped her face in my hands, smoothing her hair and staring into her beautiful blue eyes.

I could've lived in this moment forever.

17

In the beginning, things were easy.

Staci would leave cute love-notes hidden around my apartment, in my kitchen drawers, and in my books; things like, "You're so cute when you sleep," and "I heart your face, love bug." They were silly, but to me, they were refreshing reminders of genuine affection. They made me feel a little less monstrous and more like a person again; a quality I think I had been missing for some time now.

Three weeks after meeting, we were booked together again; only this time we weren't having sex with each other. Instead, we played an estranged couple, her character having a secret affair.

That was also the day I met James Deen. I'll never forget sitting in the makeup room, listening to Staci's moans echo from down the hall as he fucked her senseless. I was suddenly reminded of what Allie had said to me all those months ago about sex between partners no longer feeling sacred when it's sold to strangers. I felt empty.

"He said he wants to shoot me for his website," Staci said, giddy on the ride home.

"He's an asshole," I said.

"What's your problem?" she said.

"He'll probably try and fuck you off-camera."

"So what?"

"I don't want you working with him again."

"You can't tell me who I can or can't work with."

"I'm your *boyfriend.*"

"And he's *James Deen.*"

"Fuck James Deen.

"No, Fuck you."

This continued with compounding hostility in every demand, protest, and antagonization. Soon she started leaving fewer and fewer notes, and the ones she would leave were joyless, somber signs of fleeting love. "I don't know where to go from here," she tacked on my dresser mirror, and "Please don't forget about me," she hid in my set bag, taped to my bottle of pills. My work ethic was tanking as a result; I was too clouded—too fucking confused.

Staci's demeanor changed; she became irritable, bad-tempered, her eyes sullen and her skin nicotine yellow. I noticed recurring patches of purple bruises scattered across her body.

"They were just rough with me at work," she said. "Don't worry about it."

"Babe, your body is covered. You look anemic."

"Just leave me alone!" she said, bolting into the bathroom and locking herself inside. This wasn't the first time.

She began disappearing in there for what seemed like hours at a time, sneaking away, I thought, to text or call someone else—a secret lover, perhaps. But then I found crumpled pieces of burnt tinfoil in the trashcan or tossed on the tile floor, and a sour stench like burning plastic always sat in the air.

I confronted her about it, and after another shouting match, I noticed something off, something alarming.

"Come here," I said. "Open your mouth."

"What?" she said, defensive but compliant. She opened wide, giving me a clear look at her teeth, or at least what was left of them.

"The backs of your teeth," I said. "They're *black*."

She quickly cupped her mouth. "Fuck you," she said, running back into the bathroom, her safe haven, her hideaway.

It was worse than I thought. I did some research and learned that *users* will heat the tin foil in an effort to liquefy the drug before smoking it. And the rotting teeth were a side effect called *meth-mouth*.

Just hearing the words made my stomach turn.

It took some persistence, but she eventually owned up to it. I had never dealt with addiction before. I couldn't read the signs, and didn't know what steps to take. I tried my best to keep her clean, but I was weak and impatient. She resented me for it. I let my sweet peach decay right in front of my eyes.

In the end, there was no hope for us. I couldn't find the words needed to convince her to stay, but then again, maybe I had just given up; you can't fight for someone when your heart isn't in it, especially if they don't want to be saved.

Like most of the other women in my life, Staci moved on and found someone new, never to be seen or heard from again.

18

Feeling low, I was back at the Winnetka house with the cool kids. I knew it was a bad idea, but I let them talk me into taking shrooms.

Gavin lay shirtless on the couch, rubbing his abs, his eyes half closed but his gaze fixed on Fiona, who slithered on the living room floor, tugging at her shirt and fingering the lip of her jeans. Chester was also on the floor—isolated in a corner, wrapped in a blanket and sitting cross-legged on top of a pillow, his palms up and his chakras aligned.

I remained on the other couch, curled in the fetal position awaiting the inevitable. And when it came, I felt tense, uneasy, and afraid--like the first time all over again. The room started crushing, and I bugged out. I ran into the bathroom to collect myself. I tried to shit but I couldn't. I tried to throw up, but I couldn't bring myself to stick my fingers far enough down my throat. At a loss, I turned off the lights and laid in the bathtub, desperate for peace. Weezy scurried in underneath the door and sat on top of the toilet, watching me, studying and silently judging. I couldn't handle his beady red eyes so I went back out to the living room. Gavin was now doing pushups, Fiona was dancing like the inflatable woman, and Chester was still secluded in the corner, his eyes shut tight with a stern look of mediation on his face.

Panic. Hot flashes. I ran outside to the front stoop, but the blaring horns and obnoxious lights of the passing traffic kept me restless. I had no choice but to go back inside, returning to the couch while Gavin and Fiona laced up their gloves and stepped into the ring. Much like Staci and I, the two of them had reached their breaking point.

Fiona was also feeling spooked, but her fear manifested itself outwardly. While sweating and pacing the living room she whined, "I need to stand up, no, I need to lie down, *no*, I need to smoke, NO! I need some water."

"Can't you just be still?" Gavin said. "Quit fidgeting, dammit."

"I'm just cold," she said, grabbing a blanket, and then tossing it away, "No I'm overheated. Christ, I can't think straight!"

"Just sit down and be quiet," Gavin barked.

"Don't tell me what to do, asshole," she said.

"Guys, please!" Chester begged. "I can't focus when you fight."

"Oh, fuck off," Gavin said.

"Do you have any coke?" Fiona asked. "Please! I need something to get me straight."

"Ha! And you call *me* an addict?" Gavin said. "Look

at you!"

"Fuck you," she said. "I know where you keep it. I'll get it myself."

And as she walked off toward Gavin's bedroom, he gave chase. "Get the fuck out of my room, bitch!" He yelled, punching the walls and kicking the door.

This was unbearable. I was done. I had to leave this place. I closed my eyes and centered my breathing, succumbing to the induced visuals in my mind. In an instant I was shot into hyperspace, a million bright lights whirling past my face. I was moving fast, almost too fast to handle, but I wasn't afraid. I barreled toward pulsing phosphorescence. The light enveloped me, washing over my body and swallowing me whole.

This was it, me getting what I deserved, my breath shallow and my heart stopping. This was the end.

My eyes burst open, the wind rushing back into my lungs. I grabbed my chest, amazed to find that I was still here, still alive.

And just like the passing of a nightmare, everything slowly came back into focus and returned back to normal—well, some semblance of normal, anyway. The arguing continued and Chester remained stoic, but thankfully, my trip was fading. I had defeated the demon.

I got a glass of water and sat at the dining room table, taking notice of an old notebook half buried under discarded mail and shopping receipts. I leafed through it; all the pages were blank. I assumed it must've been a notebook someone had bought with the intention of writing the great American novel, but had then gotten high and forgotten all about it.

Holding the notebook in my hand, I now had a sudden urge to use it, so I found a pen and started writing. I wrote about the moment, my surroundings, my feelings, my mistakes, my fears, the girls I fucked, the girls I fucked over, the money I earned and the money I pissed away. I wrote about the drugs I'd done, the scenes I shot, the friends I'd made, and the love I'd lost. I escaped by purging onto the page, constructing shields out of sentences and castles out of paragraphs; the power of writing offering me immunity.

By sunrise, I had written almost a hundred pages in longhand. It was the beginning of a story—my story: the misadventures of a male performer.

19

Predictably, Gavin and Fiona broke up again. "For good this time," he assured me as a rail of white disappeared up his nose. His partying intensified. He started inviting me out almost every night of the week. I got tired of constantly telling him, no, so I stopped picking up the phone. Soon it stopped ringing altogether.

I later heard through the rumor mill that his budding coke habit landed him in some trouble at work. Allegedly, he lost wood on a *Brazzers* set and couldn't rebound. The director had no choice but to fire him, but Gavin refused to leave. He went mad, flipping the craft table, ripping open douches, and pouring out bottles of lube, leading to his immediate "removal" from set. I never did bother to ask for his side of the story.

Fiona quit the business shortly after breaking up with Gavin. Last I heard she moved to Oregon and got herself involved in some scheme where she'd be paid ten grand to marry an Icelandic immigrant so he could legally get his green card. Here I thought that was something that only happened in the movies.

Once the couple split, Chester couldn't afford to pay rent anymore, so he found himself a cramped studio apartment over the hill in pits of East Hollywood. In an effort to clear his mind, he devoted most of his time to the study of ascension through the use of psychedelics. He started tripping on such a regular basis that he rarely left the house anymore. When he wasn't crossing the planes, he was pouring over a canvas, the skin of his hands stained a permanent black from compulsively sketching his charcoal skulls.

And me, well, I kept my head down and concentrated on work, keeping my mind focused and my income steady. No more mock-relationships or drugs—at least nothing *too* heavy. That chapter in my life had come to a close, and this quickly translated into seeing less and less of the cool kids until they too became nothing more than just a fleeting memory.

A YEAR

01

I was on a red-eye back home for Christmas, seated by the aisle of the very last row, right next to the bathrooms—just in case.

See, I have a highly irrational and absurdly improbable fear of flying. Something about being strapped inside of an air-sealed 75-ton tin can, and the immediate future of my existence being left in the hands of a complete stranger at 35,000 feet doesn't bode well with me. No matter how many times I do it, I always think this time will be the last.

I tried distracting my overactive imagination by blazing through Stephen King's, On Writing—just one of the new books I recently picked up to help give me perspective on the craft. I read as King recounted his near-fatal car crash that broke his hip and collapsed his lung.

The plane bounced. My stomach dropped and my hands left greasy imprints on the book covers. Nausea set in, and I breathed through my mouth, swallowing between each breath to make sure my guts stayed where they belonged.

I put down the book and closed my eyes, focusing on

happy thoughts, thinking of home and what I hoped to find when I got there. My dad always took the holidays seriously, often going a bit overboard with the decorations—our house always the brightest and most festive on the block. Inside, the fireplace would crackle, warming the house as the smell of pine permeated the air. The Christmas tree would twinkle, and below it would lay endless gifts of all shapes and sizes. In the kitchen would be tin containers stacked high, overflowing with homemade chocolate chips cookies and pizzelles, or "pitzels"—as it read on my Nana's secret family recipe.

These thoughts (along with two Ambien) soothed me enough to induce sleep for the duration of the flight.

My parent's nightly routine was almost as strict as their morning, so they were already in bed, fast asleep long before I got home. I was greeted by a dark driveway, the decorations up but unlit. Inside, the Christmas tree stood tall, but it was barren.

The kitchen still held promise; the tins were loaded with a fresh batch. I ate two handfuls of cookies and drank 2% straight from the gallon while standing in front of the open refrigerator.

I went downstairs into the basement. The boo-box was still there, and it was still blood red but it now sported two plush cushions on top, leading a new life as a bench.

Bloated, and still feeling the effects from the Ambien, I fell asleep fully clothed on top of the very same bed where I lost my virginity all those years ago.

In the morning, my dad left for work at 6:00 a.m. like he always did; even during the holidays he never got much of a break. My mom, on the other hand, had a two-week vacation. Her and I sat in the dining room and talked over coffee.

"So, how's LA treating you?" she asked.

"Eh, it's fine," I said.

"And work? It's going well?"

"Yeah, as well as it could be. I'm making good money."

"You know if you ever want to come back home, the door's open."

"*Mom…*"

"We just worry, honey. I pray for you every night."

"Mom, stop! Please, I'm okay. I promise."

"We love you."

"I love you too. But you don't have worry."

"We just want to make sure you're healthy and clean, and—"

"Mom, come on, let's not talk about this right now, everything's fine, okay?" I changed tact. "So, why isn't the tree decorated yet?" I asked.

"We were waiting for you," she said. "We know how much you enjoy doing it."

"I do, that's nice of you. You mind if I start it?"

"Sure, but wait until Dad gets home to do the star."

"That's his favorite part," I said, heading into the living room to unpack the ornaments.

02

Christmas day.

Joey and his family came over to open presents and have dinner. Joey was now thirty-two and worked as a construction project manager. He was married with two kids, Kayla and Michelle. Stephanie, his wife, worked as a nurse just like our mom. The two of them owned their first home together less than ten minutes down the street.

Before dinner, Joey and I went on a walk to work up an appetite.

"I know it's probably nothing like the stuff you've been getting in Cali," he said, lighting a small one-hitter. "But it'll still get you high."

"I don't even think you and I ever shared a drink together," I said, taking the piece and lighting it. "And now we're smoking a bowl on Christmas."

"Yeah, well, times change," he said. "Speaking of which, don't fucking let Steph know we smoked pot because she'll beat my ass."

Oh yeah, times had definitely changed.

Joey reached into his coat pocket and pulled out a book-sized rectangle wrapped in brown paper. "I had this thing planned; kinda just wanna get it out of the way." He handed me the gift. "I thought it'd be pretty funny to do some sort of passing of the torch, but I got a feeling you've already seen this once or twice."

I ripped away the paper. Inside was a relic of the past. The black plastic completely unmarked, without a single trace of identity, and yet, I knew it was the one, the tape that changed my life forever.

"You're kidding me," I said. "Is this what I think it is?"

"Depends. What do you think it is?"

"Dude, this is that fucking porno, isn't it?"

"Oh, so you *have* seen it?"

"How the hell did you know?"

"Because I knew my brother was a snoopy little asshole."

"Oh yeah?" I said. "Man, This is great. I can't believe you still had this."

"Yeah, well, don't do something stupid and forget it at home for mom to accidentally watch."

"And what would she watch it with? They threw away the VCR years ago."

"All right, smart ass, you know what I mean."

"Yeah, yeah. Don't you worry, I'll keep it safe."

"So, yeah, everyone knows what you're doing, and it's

cool; I don't give a shit. So long as you're getting paid and you're not hurting anybody, you can do whatever you want as far as I'm concerned. I just ask you to please do me one favor, one very small favor, okay? Just stay the fuck out of my porn searches, please? I don't need to see *you* while I'm doing *that*, all right?"

"Got it. I'll do my best."

"Great," he said. "Now lets go eat, huh?"

At the table, we feasted on turkey breast, ham, mac and cheese, string-bean casserole, mashed potatoes, and pumpkin pie, all made with love. My dad may handle the decorations, but my mom rules the kitchen.

Everyone discussed work at the office or at the construction site; I did my best to contribute, but I'd be lying if I said I didn't feel a little disconnected, familiar but different.

Still, it was good to be home.

03

The next day I got a call from Lou. He was now living in New York working as an editor at a postproduction house, having graduated a semester early with honors. He was hosting Bernie for the weekend and wanted me to come join them in the city. Wasting no time, I booked myself a seat on the next *Bolt Bus*.

After two hours on the road, I hailed a cab to the restaurant *Traif* where I met the guys for dinner and drinks as a pre-game before bar hopping in Brooklyn.

"This fucking guy!" said Lou as he threw his arm around me. "I can't watch porn now because of you. You've ruined it for me, you son of a bitch!"

Bernie chimed in, "Yeah, man, I go on *Pornhub*, and Bam! There's your fucking dick and your big shit eating grin right there on the front page."

"Hey, what can I say? Logan has an audience, baby."

"Goddamn right he does," said Bernie. "You're a star, my friend."

Drinks soon arrived and Lou took the floor. "Alright,

alright," he said. "I just wanna say, it's great to have the boys back together again. Cheers, guys!"

"Cheers!" We clinked glasses and took our first sips of the night.

Lou continued, "I wanna take this opportunity to make an announcement. This afternoon, I quit my job."

"You did what?" I said.

"That's right. I walked into my boss's office, dropped my company hard drive on his desk, and said my future is not editing goddamn reality TV. I'm outta here."

"What a killer," said Bernie.

I pantomimed a rifle and shot it at Lou. "Pow! Straight to the heart."

"And he just had to take it with a smile on his face?" asked Bernie.

"He didn't have much of a choice," said Lou. "Fuck him. I got something better lined up anyway. Speaking of which." Lou turned his attention to me. "You got any room on your couch?"

"Oh shit," I said. "Does that mean what I think it means?"

"The kid's coming to Hollywood, baby."

"Oh, baby!" I said. "Got plenty of room."

"You know," said Bernie. "I've been thinking about moving out West too, in the summer, after graduation, of course."

"I'll put you up too," I said. "What the hell. Bring a

sleeping bag; you can take the floor."

"Man, I'll sleep in the goddamn bathtub," he said. "So long as we get *Asa Akira* to come pay us a visit once in a while, if you know what I mean."

"Personally," said Lou, "I'll take *Tori Black* any day of the week."

"I'll drink to that," I said. "Lets get a couple tequila shots to celebrate."

"The boys from Philly are taking over the West Coast!" shouted Bernie.

"This is gonna be a great fucking night," said Lou.

After dinner we got cocktails at *Iron Station* and then free slices of pizza with each beer at *American Cheez*, and then we closed out the night at *Union Hall*.

And that's where I met *Laura Smith*, a leggy blonde thirty-something, starved and on the prowl.

"I could smell the pheromones," she said to me at the bar as I ordered a Gin and Tonic—my fourth for the night, on top of two Tequila shots and three beers. Needless to say, I was loose and on the verge of greatness as lights bled and the world blurred. Or maybe I was just on the brink of blacking out.

"You look familiar," she said. "I know you from somewhere."

"I just have one of those faces," I said.

"No, no," she persisted. "You're somebody. Your name's...*Logan*, isn't it?"

I laughed. "I don't know," I said, "maybe..."

"I had a feeling," she said, pleased with herself. She leaned forward and whispered in my ear, "Wanna know a secret? I've always wanted to fuck a Porn star."

"...Really?" I said, intrigued. "Well...now that you have one right here in front of you, what are you going to do about it?"

Laura sized me up. "I'm taking you home with me tonight," she said.

"I don't know," I said, beaming. "You might not be able to handle it."

She laughed, playfully balling my shirt in her fist. "Just pray you can keep up, kid," she said.

"A challenge," I said. "Rock and Roll."

We left the bar at 3:00 A.M. My friends were concerned for me, but I went anyway.

"I'll see you fucks tomorrow morning," I said as Laura tugged on my sleeve, pulling me outside into the street.

She led me to her basement brownstone apartment. Her two large Great Danes greeted us at the door. After locking them in their colossal crates, Laura showed me to her room and I stumbled onto her bed. She joined me and we kissed.

I rested a hand on her throat, but she stopped me. "No hands on my neck," she said.

"Oh, sorry," I mumbled, moving my hand to her shoulder.

Laura shimmied down the bed and slipped off my pants. She again swatted away my hand when it lingered near her face. She slipped on a condom and climbed on top. Penetration was warm, but the softness of her bed was too inviting to ignore. I started nodding off and my eyelids fell, much like my wood.

Laura slapped my face. "Wake up!" she said.

"Huh? What?" I said, barely coming to. "Oh, sorry...I'm so...too much drink."

"You fucking asshole," she said, pushing me away as I fell back asleep. The condom came off and was tossed to the floor. I passed out. No sex tonight.

I woke in complete darkness, forgetting where I was, who I was with, and how the hell I had gotten there. I sat up and clutched my skull. I found my clothes piled next to the bed, and as I got dressed I was overcome with dizziness. With a swift sense of urgency, I staggered around the darkness until I found the bathroom. I felt for the toilet, lifted the seat, stuck my head in the bowl, and let it out. Panting and covered in sweat, I found the sink, splashed cold water on my face, and washed out my mouth. Then I remembered where I was and what had happened. I cursed myself under my breath.

I wandered out of the bathroom and into the living room that too was cast in complete darkness. I heard the flick of a lighter and turned to see Laura sitting at her kitchen dinette smoking a cigarette, the dogs by her side.

"...Hey," I said guiltily.

"Hi," she said.

"Uh, what time is it?" I asked.

"10:00 A.M."

"Christ! Really?" I said. "Why is it so dark in here?"

"Basement apartment," she said. "No windows."

"Oh," I said, looking around and realizing there were indeed no windows at all. "Hey, I'm, uh...sorry about last night. I drank way too much."

"Shit happens," she said. "It's whatever. You want some coffee?"

"No, that's fine," I said. "I should probably go."

"There's the door," she said, smoke dancing as she waved her finger.

"Right. Well, it was nice meeting you."

"Uh huh."

I made my exit and stepped outside, both blinded by the harsh morning sunlight and deafened by the piercing screeches of passing cars and the perpetual construction of the city. Nothing compares to the noise of New York, especially while nursing a hangover and a deflated ego. I sat on the stoop of Laura's building and called an Uber back to Lou's.

Welcoming me inside he said, "Ladies and gentlemen, the millennial porn star has returned! What do you say, kid, did you slay her?"

"I definitely left my mark," I said.

"That'a boy," said Lou, patting my shoulder and

heading into the kitchen.

I followed and found Bernie manning the stove. "I gotta feast planned for us. Eggs, Pork roll, and Bacon," he said, everything already sizzling in the pan.

I took a whiff and my stomach turned. "Hey Lou," I said, "where's your bathroom?"

He pointed toward the hallway and I rushed out of the kitchen. I closed the bathroom door, curled over the toilet bowl and heaved. I again washed my mouth out at the sink, and when I opened the door, Lou was standing there waiting.

"It happens to the best of us," he said, handing me a glass of water.

"Man, I feel like shit," I said. "I think I'm just gonna catch the bus back home."

"Gotta do what you gotta do," he said.

"I hope you're serious about coming back to California," I said.

"Don't worry," he said, hi-fiving me. "I'll be there."

"Me too!" Bernie called out from the kitchen. "Don't you dare forget about me."

"Ha, never!" I said. "Looking forward to it."

I said my goodbyes and headed home.

04

On the bus, I thought about the past: losing my virginity, high school blues, teenage drama, and my predictions for life after college. But mainly I thought about Allie. I imagined what our future could have been like had we stayed together. I wondered how this trip home would have been different had I been coming to see her. We would've spent Christmas morning together opening presents at my parent's house. Then she would've been in the kitchen helping my mom with dinner or dancing around the house with the girls; they adored her. She's going to make a great mother some day.

I found Allie's number in my phone, my thumb lingering over the call button. It had been nearly six months since we last spoke, but in my mind we had had a million conversations; I had been seeing her in the face of every girl I met.

I pressed the button and took a deep breath. The phone rang twice before her soft voice answered.

"...Hello," she said.

"Hey..."

"Hey."

I fumbled. "Uh, you know who this, I mean, you still have my number, right?"

"Of course. How are you?"

"Oh, I'm great," I said. "I just wanted to call and say what's up? Merry Christmas, by the way."

"Merry Christmas. You come home to see your family?"

"Yeah, to see everybody, really."

"How are they?"

"They're doing well. Dad's still working everyday, and Mom panics about everything."

She giggled. "Did you see Joe? How are the girls?"

"Oh yeah, they came over for dinner. They are like little adults now. They were asking about you."

"Oh, god, they are too cute! I miss them. So, how long are you staying?"

"I leave tomorrow morning."

"That's a short stay."

"Yeah, well…that's kind of the reason I'm calling. Since I'm leaving so soon, I don't know, I was kind of wondering if we could, you know, see each other?"

"…You know I've been dating someone, right?"

"Oh. Actually, I didn't know that. Well, I don't mean anything big, just like a coffee or something so we could talk for a minute. I just…have a lot I want to say to you, and I think if we're in person it would be better. I miss you. I don't mean like *that*, I just miss talking to you."

"…I don't think that's a good idea."

"Why not? I mean, you don't have to come to me, I have my parent's car, I can meet you anywhere."

"No. Look, Sean knows of you and knows we dated for a while. He's been having a tough time dealing with it."

"Dealing with what? I don't understand."

"The fact that I dated a porn star."

"Are you serious?"

"I'm sorry, but he made me promise—"

"Promise not to see me?"

"Yeah."

"And promise not to talk to me too, I bet."

"Something like that."

"…Should I delete your number?"

"I don't think you should call me again."

"…I get it. "

"I'm sorry. I should probably go."

"Uh-huh."

"…Bye."

"Bye."

05

On my last night home, I ran the shower and sat on the floor of my parent's hall bathroom with my laptop perched on the toilet seat in front of me; just like old times, like I had never grown up and left. Only now I was watching my own porn, seeing myself at my finest: stark naked with a raging hard-on, balls deep inside of an insatiable fuck doll.

And in those few short moments of orgasm, I experienced clarity. I saw myself from outside, floating high above my body. I could see my younger-self going through these exact motions, wishing one day he could be that guy— That cock on the screen.

I had done it. I actualized the fantasy and achieved the dream. I was now on millions of computer screens all across the world. Guys would give *anything* to live a day of my life.

But what did I have to show for it? Who had I become now that I was officially on the front pages of tube sites?

Who is Logan?

That's what I still needed to figure out. These

experiences and these exploits could no longer be in vain, instead they would have to serve as vital steps on my road to self-discovery.

06

The Hard Rock Hotel in Las Vegas is home to the A.V.N. (Adult Video Network) expo; the four-day long convention/ exhibition where studios hawk their products and agencies promote their talent. Everyone who's anyone gets a booth, and lines wraparound for autographs from superstars like Julia Anne, Kendra Lust, and Lou and Bernie's personal favorites: Tori Lane and Asa Akira.

In my hotel room on the fifth floor of the Paradise Tower, I gazed out of the window toward the strip as I knotted my polka dot periwinkle tie, which matched my periwinkle shirt I had buttoned under my sleek grey suit. I was getting ready for the crux of A.V.N. weekend: the award ceremony, otherwise known as, "The Oscars of Porn."

I was even nominated for an award.

The category: **Best Male Newcomer**.

Since my departure from the cool kids and after having hit the skids on any romantic pursuits, I planned to go stag to the red carpet with only my friend, *Stella Artois*, by my side. But after giving it some thought, I figured, what the hell, if I'm going to be a porn star, I might as well embrace the unquestionably awkward situations I'm bound to have with my parents for the rest of my life and just let them experience the fray for themselves. I bought them round-trip flights to Vegas and put them up in the Luxor hotel for the weekend with spa packages and tickets to the award show, all under one condition: they had to be my dates on the red carpet. My first would be their first.

They met me in the lobby, and together the three of us walked arm in arm, smiling big for all the cameras to adore. Most people seemed a little confused, like they had never seen a boy with his parents before at the porn awards, but I didn't care; tonight was my night. Afterward, my parents wished me luck and set off upstairs to find their balcony seats. I went to the bar and grabbed two beers before taking my seat in the fourth row, the nominee section; the place where I could be called to take the stage and deliver a speech, declaring my official arrival into the world of porn.

Soon the lights dimmed and the show began. Host and fellow swordsman, *Pete Pistol*, sang a show tune about his unfaltering ability to get wood. Nina Nives won "Most Outrageous Performer." Elvis Bone won "Best D.I.L.F." for his role in, "Daddy Issues 10." Then as an interlude, members of Cirque Du Soleil came on and performed an erotic aerial silk show.

Thirty minutes in and I had to piss like a racehorse, so I snuck out and headed toward the lobby bathroom. En route, my ears perked as I heard a familiar voice, something shrill.

"Peeerrzzz," I heard it say. I turned and saw my old fling and walking contagion, Nikki Sinn, camping out in front of the woman's bathroom, nodding heavily against the wall. "Well, well," she said, stumbling towards me. "If it isn't my little fuck-boy."

"Oh, Jesus," I said under my breath as she reached her hands around my head and pulled my face to her tits.

"Yeah, you miss those, don't you, you pervert?" she said, cackling.

I didn't fight as she grabbed my butt and slid her tongue over my cheek.

"You don't have any blow, do you?" she said. "They just released me three days ago and I'm looking to celebrate."

"Released?" I asked.

"From jail, motherfucker."

"You're always in trouble, aren't you?"

"Some *fucker* keyed my car, so I went crazy on him and his bitch," she said. "Not my fault. Whatever, I need a smoke, you at least have some fucking cigarettes on you?"

I shook my head. "Sorry."

She pressed herself closer. "All you're good for is your *dick*—Hey!" she yelled, craning her neck toward a passerby. "I see you, bitch. Don't think I'm not watching."

The girl called back, "I know you ain't talking to me."

Taking the opportunity, I ducked into the bathroom.

"See-ya, Nikki," I said.

I heard her call out, "Hey, don't you walk away—" but the bathroom door closed before I figured out which one of us she was talking to. Thankfully, it stayed shut, and I figured I was safe.

I pissed and took an extra minute washing my hands to ensure a clean exit. I peered outside. Nikki was gone and I didn't see any mobile security, so I took the opportunity to go back to the bar to refuel. It was packed with a sea of thirsty porn stars, mopes, and the media, all clamoring for the bartender's attention, guys throwing wads of cash and girls flashing their tits. Sheer Pandemonium. The bartender was both the most loved and loathed man in the room. Finally, I made my way to the front and got his attention, and not wanting to make another trip, I ordered two more *Stellas*.

A hand patted my shoulder. It was Chester.

"Broseph!" he said.

"Chester, what's up, man?" I said, giving him a hug. "How the hell are you?"

"Getting there," he said. "Getting there. Hey, congratulations, by the way."

"Congratulations for what?" I asked.

"Bro, you just fucking won."

"What?"

"Look," he said, pointing to one of the live-feed TV's behind the bar.

I turned and saw on the screen a projection with a

picture of my face and the words emblazoned across, "Winner, Best Male Newcomer: Logan Pierce."

"No way," I said, stunned.

The bartender returned, "Two beers," he said. "That'll be twenty bucks."

Breaking my stare, I handed him my card and then looked back at the TV. As quickly as it had appeared, my face was now gone, replaced by a new picture of a new winner. The show must go on, after all.

"Shit," I said. "I probably should've been up there."

"It doesn't matter," said Chester. "They reduced the awards to a slide show after forty minutes so now they're just rattling them off."

"Is that normal?"

"Yeah, that's how it is every year. That's porn. Anyway, congratulations, man. It was good seeing you."

"Thanks. Yeah, you too. See you around."

We shook hands and I texted my parents, telling them to meet me outside the ballroom.

"Hey, so what do you know about that?" my dad said, going in for a hug. "Best Male Newcomer."

"There you are!" said my mom. "We were so excited. Why didn't you go on stage?"

"I was at the bar," I said. "I kinda missed the announcement."

"It was so nice anyway, they had your picture and everything," my mom said.

"So, Logan Pierce, huh?" my dad said. "Not such a bad name."

"We saw Ron Jeremy," my mom said, "He's a lot fatter in real life."

"Tell me about it," I said.

My dad yawned and checked his watch. "I think we're going to head back to the hotel and get some sleep," he said. "It's after ten."

"*Way* past our bedtime," my mom said.

"No problem," I said, hugging them goodbye. "I'll talk to you guys tomorrow."

I was half ready to go to the Hard Rock diner, get myself a celebratory slice of Apple pie with melted cheddar cheese on top, and then head back to my room, but fate had other plans from me.

I got a text from Becky Bolt. It read, "Hey award winner. Got another bottle of Cab. Wanna celebrate?"

Decisions, decisions.

I texted her back and she met me in front of the elevators. Upstairs, the door closed and she pushed me to the bed. Climbing on top, she pulled my shirt up over my face and pinned my arms to the bed.

"Don't fucking move," she warned, softly kissing my lips and grazing her fingernails across my cheek. She moved below to my chest and kissed my nipples and my abs, working lower, undoing my belt, my button, and my zipper.

She removed my shirt from my face and replaced it

with her fishnet-clad foot. "Suck it," she said. I obeyed, licking and worshipping as she thrust it in and out of my mouth. She straddled me. I reached my arms toward her, but she pushed them away. "I said don't fucking move."

She gripped my shaft, teasing the head on the surface of her warm slit; slowly guiding it inside, making sure we both felt every inch of its entry. She gyrated as her muscles flexed and her body spasmed. She hauled me out of bed and arched herself against the hotel room window. I joined her, pressing her face against the glass, the rest of the world residing ten-stories below.

"I want you to cum for me," she said, falling to her knees, eager for a payload, which coated her throat, glistened on her tongue, and swayed suspended from her teeth. Then, with a determined look, she pointed to the floor as if to say, *get on your fucking knees*. I complied. She leaned over me, pried my lips apart, and dropped the entirety of it into my mouth.

"Swallow it," she said.

I did as I was told. It didn't taste so bad; I actually quite liked it. How's that for a new discovery?

Becky cupped my chin and smiled in contentment. Then, as a final, *fuck you*, she slapped my face and retired to the bed, finishing up the last of the wine as I sat alone on the floor, licking my lips and reveling in the afterglow of victory.

In the morning, I treated my parents to breakfast

at Blueberry Farms—the only wholesome restaurant in Sin City. Then we went to the airport to catch our flights, them to a frigid Philadelphia and me back into the machine of Los Angeles.

A.V.N. weekend was officially over and I was now inducted into the ranks and record books; documented as an icon, a winner.

Author Jim Carroll once said, "Time sure flies when you're young and jerking off." With that in mind, I guess it would only make sense that time for me would move at a swift and incomprehensible pace. In this business, a year felt like almost nothing, like it was just a figment of my imagination, and at any second I could wake up as a different person leading a different life. But it was real, it happened, and I was there for it all.

07

The air of the room was thick from my partner and I having just worked up a sweat. We took a break so she could get a touch of make-up while I sprawled across the white leather couch, catching my breath and toweling myself dry.

A crewmember fussed with the barn doors of one of the lights. I shielded my eyes as I sat up and draped the towel over my head.

The weight of the couch shifted, my seat cushion expanding with air. I looked up to see the B-camera operator, *Marty*, crossing his leg and puffing an E-cig, a torn and faded NYU alumni cap flopped on his head.

"You ever see the film, *Logan's Run*?" he asked.

"No," I said, "but people have been saying I should."

"Every time you're on set I can't help but think of it."

The director approached, having come from the bathroom, which was doubling as the make-up studio. "She's just getting lips," he said to the group. "Back and ready in three minutes," he walked toward me. "Think you're good to go for the pop?" he asked, his phone vibrating in his pocket.

"Just need a minute to get myself close," I said.

"No problem," he said, walking off to take the call.

I ran the towel through my hair one final time and dropped it behind the couch, out of sight out of mind. I lounged back and closed my eyes. Taking a deep breath, my nostrils were flooded with whisk of artificial vanilla.

"Michael York and Farrah Fawcett," said Marty.

"What?" I asked.

"In the movie. Sci-fi, dystopian future—oh man, it's a blast."

"Hey Marty," I said. "Could you, uh, give me some space? You understand."

"Oh!" he said, jumping to his feet. "Of course, of course. Gotta get everything flowing, I get it."

"Thanks," I said, and then as an after thought, "Oh, could you do me a favor and hand me the *bucket*?"

He sighed, "...Sure."

Pinching the handle, he grabbed the (fuck) bucket and held it out for me to survey. There were a few greasy and color-coded, but unmarked squeeze bottles, a roll of cheap paper towels, and a packet of unscented baby wipes. I settled on the pink colored bottle—coconut oil. I uncapped it and squirted some into the palm of my hand.

"Thanks again," I said, plopping the bottle back.

Marty walked away and I resumed my routine, drowning out the world and substituting my own in my mind; a memory, a fantasy, anything to escape the reality of sitting naked on a dirty couch, jacking off in front of half a dozen jaded lifers, all counting the minutes until they can clock out and go home.

But this is all part of the job, just another day at the office. It's moments like this where I can't help but laugh; it's all I can do, really. I've come to realize that being a performer is very much about getting over yourself, insecurities and all. It's about checking the ego at the door and living without inhibitions, ready and willing to embrace the inner pervert at a moment's notice.

And something like that requires a brush of masochism, a dash of self-deprecation, and most importantly, a sense of humor. It's necessary if anyone hopes to survive in this business.

Just remember, at the end of the day, it's only porn.

thank you

Mom, Dad, Rob and Missy for all your love and support. Sasha for being my love and my muse. Lucas for being a godsend. Ryan, Joey, and Kyle—the Justice League. Matt R. for being such a sucker for movies. Matt L., Rob H., Dan H., Rob C., Amy, David, Dan C., Samantha, and Jessica for the read-throughs and for being my sounding boards. Lou, the legend, for always offering a solution. Ashley for the two years. Quyen, Natasha, Abi, Carly, and Morgan for the memories. Theo for the Bukowski. Jacky St. James and Chris Zeischegg for the quotes. Derric for the transcriptions. Ben for allowing me to be his first. Michael, Mischa, Billy, Cameron, Maia, Dana, Chad, Carter, and the rest of my co-workers in the industry for the infinitely vast pool of inspiration. And finally, to Dirk Diggler for always rockin' and rollin.'

about the author

J.R. Verlin is a writer living in Los Angeles, and for the better part of a decade, he has been gracing box covers and front pages of X-rated Tube sites across the world as his lascivious alter ego, Logan Pierce.

Further reading at Whoislogan.com

Logan Pierce
22024 Lassen St,
#114,
Clatsworth, CA
91311 - USA

Made in the USA
San Bernardino, CA
13 May 2019